The Complete Guide to Christian Coach Training

2012 Edition

LINDA C. HEDBERG

Scripture references found in this book are used with permission of the publishers referenced below.

Scripture quotations marked "NLT" are taken from the Holy Bible, New Living Translation, copyright 1996. Used by permission of Tyndale House Publishers, Inc., Wheaton, Illinois 60189. All rights reserved.

Scripture quotations marked "NIV" are taken from HOLY BIBLE, NEW INTERNATIONAL VERSION®. Copyright © 1973, 1978, 1984 by International Bible Society. Used by permission of Zondervan Publishing House.

Scripture taken from the HOLY BIBLE, TODAY'S NEW INTERNATIONAL VERSION®. TNIV®. Copyright © 2001, 2005 by International Bible Society. Used by permission of Zondervan. All rights reserved worldwide.

The Message. Copyright © 1993, 1994, 1995, 1996, 2000, 2001, 2002. Used by permission of NavPress Publishing Group.

Scripture quotations marked "KJV" are taken from the Holy Bible, King James Version, Cambridge, 1769.

The prayer on page 76 is used by permission from *Christ-Centered Coaching: 7 Benefits for Ministry Leaders*, by Jane Creswell, Chalice Press, www.chalicepress.com.

The information presented on training and professional organizations are, of course, subject to change at the discretion of the coach training organizations and are only representative of the information available at the time this book was compiled. This includes certification or credentialing requirements and the cost of tuition, for examples. The reader of the Complete Guide to Christian Coach Training is responsible for verifying all information of interest directly with the respective organizations.

Printed in the United States of America

First Printing: October 2011

ISBN – 13: 978-1466454408
ISBN - 1466454407

Table of Contents

Thank you!

I'm grateful for the support and efforts of many old friends and new, for treasured contributions to this project...

to all the coaching training program directors and assistants who have joined this project

to Tony Stoltzfus for taking the time to simply reach out and connect - resulting in a conversation that ignited the project

to Gary R. Collins for inspiration and wisdom shared with the Christian coaching community and for support and encouragement of this project

to Beth Cole for consistently fabulous logo crafting and design work

to Susan Fleming for phenomenal technical and administrative contributions and for bringing her creativity and balance to the project (www.electronicmarketingsuccess.com)

to Karen Hedberg for excellent editing skills and generous sisterly support

Finally, I'm grateful for Judy Santos, a mentor and friend, who stepped into her joy in heaven on March 2, 2010. Judy contributed her insight and cheerleading to the first two editions of this book. I miss her very much.

Thank you, Jesus, for being our grace and truth.

INTRODUCTION

*Eight years ago when I began searching for coach training, **I could have used help**.*

Identifying the available training programs was just the beginning. It wasn't easy to compare options because **I found that programs were vastly different.** They were offered at significant price differences. I noticed that programs were delivered differently. Some were virtual (over the phone, for example) and others were in person. The curriculum varied from program to program. Numerous decision-making factors surfaced and the process actually became complicated.

Fortunately, after doing a lot of research, talking to many people and receiving God's guidance through the process, I found the program that was the right match for me.

Your process can be much simpler than mine was.

I have created ***The Complete Guide to Christian Coach Training*** to streamline your process. I've done the research for you!

The Complete Guide to Christian Coach Training will provide you with all you need to jump-start and sustain your process. You will have the **information you need**, consolidated and organized to facilitate the best decisions you can make - the ones that are right for you.

An **easy-reference list** of Christian coach training programs, profiles on each program (submitted by the programs) and a comparison table for quick reference is at your fingertips.

Bottom line, instead of spending time and frustration researching and wondering if you've missed a major component, you will have more time to pray about your decision and **focus on God's unique plan for your coach training.**

The Word became flesh

and made his dwelling among us.

We have seen his glory,

the glory of the one and only Son

who came from the Father,

full of grace and truth.

John 1:14 (TNIV)

SECTION ONE: INTRODUCTION TO COACHING

COACHING DEFINED

In his ground-breaking book, *Christian Coaching: Helping Others Turn Potential into Reality* (2001), Christian leader Gary Collins defines coaching as "the art and practice of guiding a person or group from where they are toward the greater competence and fulfillment that they desire."

COACHING EXPANDED

Coaching is an ongoing relationship designed to forward a client's goals. The coach provides a structure and process that is dedicated to successfully meeting the agenda that the client sets. A client engages a coach because they desire to change something in themselves or their circumstances. The client believes a relationship that is focused on supporting the desired change will bring the results they want. A coach enhances and optimizes a process for a client resulting in the meaningful, significant change the client seeks.

COACHING SKILLS

A professional coach brings a specific set of skills to the coaching relationship. Basic coaching skills include the following:

- Establishing trust and rapport
- Acting as co-equal collaborator
- Practicing active listening
- Utilizing powerful questions
- Casting vision and identifying the gap
- Identifying resources and addressing obstacles
- Focusing on strengths

COACHING IN ACTION

A coaching conversation is a specific type of conversation that is not about giving advice. According to Tony Stoltzfus, coach trainer and author of *Leadership Coaching: The Disciplines, Skills and Heart of a Christian Coach* (2005), coaching conversations are based on the premise that "the best way to help you change is to create a structured, supportive relationship that helps you take responsibility for your life and make the changes you want to make." Coaching students can expect their professional coach instructors to train them to avoid advice-giving while helping clients take responsibility to move toward and achieve their own desired change.

COACHING IS NOT ...

Coaching students can also expect their instructors to train them to avoid taking on un-coachable clients or those best served by working with a professional counselor. Coaching is not counseling. A professional coach works with reasonably healthy, resourceful, capable clients on moving toward positive goals that result in enhancing or optimizing their lives. Unlike coaches, professional counselors are trained and licensed to help clients experiencing emotional and mental health issues. Counselors typically help clients resolve debilitating issues of the past, whereas coaches help clients focus on goals for the future. Coaching is also distinctly different from consulting, spiritual direction, mentoring, discipleship and pastoral care.

Please refer to the Life Coaching Comparison Tool on page 5 for a table that clarifies these distinctions.

The Life Coaching Comparison Tool

Presented by Linda Hedberg, CLC | Christian Coaching Resources | www.christiancoachingresources.com | 763.780.8508

	Life Coaching	Counseling or Therapy	Consulting	Spiritual Direction	Mentoring and Discipleship
Typical Relationship	One-on-One or group in a professional context	One-on-One or group in a professional context	One-on-One or organizational in a professional context	One-on-One or group in a professional or ministry context	One-on-One in a business context (mentoring) or ministry or personal context (mentoring or discipleship)
Focus	Future, vision	Past, pain	Project or problem	God	Teaching by example
Desired Outcome	Action toward meaningful goals	Healing and restoration	Expert opinion and recommendations	God's direction	Personal or spiritual growth and maturity
Training	Professional training and certification available and commonly expected	Professional training and licensing typically required	Training specific to consultant's area of expertise is commonly expected	Professional training and certification available	Not typically expected
Meetings	Often by phone, sometimes in person	In person	Usually in person	In person	Usually in person
Role	Coach is a collaborator who provides structure and process to an agenda set by the client	Counselor provides clinical expertise and facilitates a healing process	Consultant is an expert who analyzes a problem or project and provides reports and recommendations	Spiritual director is a collaborator who prays and listens with clients	Mentor or disciple is a companion who has "gone before" and can lead and advise by example

Though there is certainly overlap in the descriptions of all of the above relationships, it is helpful to identify the distinctives. Ministers involved in Pastoral Care commonly draw from aspects of each of the roles described above.

Coaching Brief History

During the 80's and 90's the field of coaching emerged from three influences - the executive and business consulting industry, the field of counseling and psychotherapy, and the personal growth movement. Thomas Leonard (1955 -2003), known as the "father of coaching," was influential in the early days of the profession, as he founded Coach U, participated in the formation of what is today the International Coach Federation, and proliferated his notoriety by establishing Coachville. With current membership at over 17,000 worldwide, The International Coach Federation (ICF) is the oldest (established in 1994) and most influential professional association of coaches. Another professional association that has gained prominence since 2003 is the International Association of Coaches (IAC).

Christian Coaching

All of the above is relevant to the field of Christian coaching, but for Christian coaches there is more, of course! Many coaches who are Christians work in organizations or in their own businesses and do not identify themselves as "Christian coaches." Often they will describe themselves as called to being salt and light in a dark world (Matthew 5: 13-14). Other coaches refer to themselves as "Christian coaches" and make that very clear in their businesses or ministries. Typically they work with Christian clients and see themselves as providing coaching to strengthen the body of Christ (1 Corinthians 12: 12-27).

"You are the salt of the earth...
You are the light of the world..."
Matthew 5:13-14 (NIV)

"All of you together are Christ's body,
and each of you is a part of it."
1 Corinthians 12:17 (NLT)

Christian coaches have been involved since the early days of the coaching profession. Jane Creswell, MCC, organized the first Christian prayer breakfast at the 1999 Annual ICF Conference, with about 12 attending. Here's what Jane says about the annual prayer breakfasts at ICF:

> ***I actually felt God prompting*** *me to do the prayer breakfast starting in 1998 and I ignored it. And was miserable. So when 1999's ICF conference was announced, I got busy organizing and dealing with lots of rejection. We've had these breakfasts at every conference since 1999 and even in other countries: Switzerland, Japan, Canada, Spain and Italy. We are usually in some back corner and our signs for the location are often removed from the bulletin board, etc. Even with those challenges, people find us and we pray. God has used this group in different ways each year to pray.*

At the 2011 ICF Conference in Las Vegas, Nevada, Christian coaches met for two breakfasts. Susan Whitcomb, PCC, coordinated the gatherings and here's what she had to say:

> *Although the group represented a variety of coaching niches (corporate, executive, global leadership, life, nonprofit, business, ministry, career, and more) from multiple countries around the globe, we shared a common spirit. On the first morning, each person offered a favorite scripture and insight that related to coaching. On the second morning, we individually shared the God-size vision for our work as coaches so that everyone could support one another in praying for that. It was encouraging to see how God has strategically planted His children around the globe to make a kingdom difference.*

The Christian Coaches Network was founded in 1998 by Judy Santos, MCC (1942 - 2010), with 18 members in the first year. In 2001, Ruth Ledesma published *Coaching by the Book*, in which members of the Christian Coaches Network contributed chapters. In 2003 the first Christian Coaches Network conference was held in Virginia Beach, Virginia (USA). The conference attracted members from across North America and included international members from the UK and Germany. Those in attendance represented a variety of coaching niches, church denominations and professional and ministry backgrounds.

Well-known author, counselor and Christian coaching pioneer Gary R. Collins' book *Christian Coaching: Helping Others Turn Potential into Reality* was originally released in 2001. Published by a major publishing house (NavPress), this book brought Christian coaching to the shelves of Christian bookstores and began to broadly educate the Christian community about the discipline, practice and newly emerging field of Christian coaching.

Within the last decade, Christian coach training organizations have been launched. In 2003, the Christian Track at the Institute for Life Coach Training (ILCT) became the first Christian coach training to be accredited by ICF. Currently, several Christian coach training programs are accredited by ICF. Graduate schools are now offering degrees specializing in coaching, including three profiled in this book.

To learn which programs have been awarded ICF accreditation, refer to the profiles on pages 31-70. Other Christian programs are currently pursuing accreditation or plan to in the near future. Still others do not intend to pursue ICF accreditation. Some report either that ICF accreditation is just simply not a part of their vision or that they disagree with the pursuit of accreditation by a secular organization.

Today, classic coaching has moved into local churches as well as denominations.

- Tennessee Baptist Convention established The Center for Christian Coaching in 2008 "to develop, coordinate, and deliver quality coaching and coach training" within their organization. For more information: http://www.tbccoaching.org/
- In 2011, after several years of various successful coaching initiatives, The Assemblies of God organized an internal network of coaches to include professional-level training and certification available for those within the denomination. For more information: http://agcoaching.org/
- Bethel Church in Redding, California, offers four levels of coach training and options for coaching ministry niche training, mostly in a workshop format. For more information: http://www.coachingworkshops.net/?cat=19/

Seven Introductory Coaching Resources

1. ***Christian Coaching: Helping Others Turn Potential into Reality* by Gary R. Collins.** This is the classic book on Christian coaching - a very informative introduction to the field. Collins' book has been a standard recommendation to prospective and new Christian coaches since it was first published in 2001. The second edition was released in 2009. Available at www.ChristianCoachingBook.com.

2. ***A Crash Course in Christian Coaching* DVD or CD by Christopher McCluskey.** This resource (2007) brings a thorough up-to-date overview of the profession to the video screen. Christian coaching pioneer, Christopher McCluskey, delivers an interesting, informative primer on the field. Available at www.christian-living.com/crash.

3. **The International Coach Federation (ICF)** is the oldest and largest professional association of coaches worldwide. Though not a distinctly Christian organization, it has undeniably shaped the profession of coaching in our world. Learn about the profession at www.coachfederation.org.

4. **The Christian Coaches Network.** A professional association of Christian coaches which has been around since 1998. Investigate the world of Christian coaching by visiting www.christiancoaches.com.

5. **Christian Coaching Magazine.** Try this resource to learn what Christian coaches are currently discussing. CCM is a unique publication with a diverse board, reflecting the diverse community of today's Christian coaches. Go to www.christiancoachingmag.com.

6. ***Co-active Coaching: Changing Business Transforming Lives (3rd Edition) by Kimsey-House et al.*** This is a very commonly used coaching textbook. Though not a distinctly Christian book, it is often taught and studied from a Christian perspective. Available at www.amazon.com.

7. **The Christian Coaching Center.** This website features a wealth of Christian coaching information, and updates are typically added weekly. Visit frequently to learn about the world of Christian coaching. Leave questions and comments and join online communities of Christian coaches with similar interests. Go to www.christiancoachingcenter.org.

SECTION TWO: CHRISTIAN COACH TRAINING 101

Yes, there could be a class in deciphering Christian coach training. It's truly more complicated than anyone would like. This ebook exists and you are reading it - two observations that make the point.

TYPES OF COACHING

In this Guide, we are discussing "classic coaching," the type of coaching that has formed a new professional field. The new field is reflected largely by the formation of the International Coach Federation, which has existed since 1994 and has over 17,000 members internationally. Other professional organizations like the International Association of Coaches (IAC) have since emerged. Christian coaches formed a professional organization, the Christian Coaches Network, in 1998.

Following the typical road to a newly formed profession, many coach training programs have emerged, as have various "camps" regarding the definitions of coaching. This is true of both secular and Christian coach training programs. In the general professional community, ICF is the oldest and largest association and has created definitions and standards for the profession. It has also created respected standards for accrediting training programs.

You may have noticed in the Christian community the term "coaching" has many definitions and can often be distilled to mean "teach," "mentor," or "disciple." At a church this author attended, for example, all the children's workers were called "coaches." Of course, most of these "coaches" were ministering wonderfully and effectively to kids; but this use of the word "coach" is not the type of professional coaching referred to in this Guide.

Because the term "coaching" is prevalent in the Christian community - often used like a "hot" new term - it can be difficult to distinguish what Christian training is focused on professional coaching skills and practices and what is focused on utilizing some coaching skills and techniques for effective ministry. Some training experiences called "coaching," are more focused on teaching, mentoring or discipleship. Clearly, learning and applying coaching skills and techniques (or teaching, mentoring and discipleship) can be very powerful in ministry. However combining the term "coaching" with effective ministry doesn't necessarily reflect the classic professional coaching referred to in this Guide.

For the purposes of this Guide, every effort has been made to identify Christian coach programs which train business and ministry professionals in classic coaching techniques. To be sure, the extent to which each program focuses on "classic" coaching and "professional-level" training can vary widely.

Types of Programs

Once a list of Christian coach training programs is identified, the differences start to become clear. Some programs focus more on training business professionals and some train ministry professionals. Programs can have various niches or specialties - like career coaching or life purpose coaching. Training for individuals is offered, while some programs can be contracted to train groups. And as previously discussed, some programs offer full professional training while others offer exposure to coaching skills.

Range of Curriculum Content

Christian coach training programs offer a range of curriculum content. Many are heavier on teaching the integration and application of Biblical and theological concepts. Others support and encourage students to individually or in small groups incorporate their faith and Biblical knowledge. Classic coaching skills are taught and examined more deeply in some programs, while others give skills overviews.

Accredited or Not

The International Coach Federation (ICF) accredits coach training programs. Nine Christian coach training programs are currently recognized by the ICF. Two are accredited as ACTP programs, four are approved as ACSTH programs, and three are approved to offer CCE courses. Refer to page 20 for a description of these three types of ICF accreditation.

The ICF accreditation process is lengthy and there is no guarantee that a program will receive accreditation. Some Christian coach training programs report that pursuing ICF accreditation is simply not a part of their vision. Other Christian programs choose not to pursue accreditation from a secular organization. You can find assistance with sorting out this decision-making factor on pages 17-26 of this Guide.

Although ICF has been around the longest, is the largest, and currently has the most influence, two other organizations that evaluate coach training have recognition in the professional coaching community. The International Association of Coaches (IAC) licenses schools that meet their standards for professional coach training. And new in 2011, the Center for Credentialing Education approves schools to provide training toward Board Certified Coach (BCC) certification.

Range of Requirements for Certification

Training programs often offer "certification" to their students for completion of certain requirements. From program to program, the requirements vary greatly. There is no current standard for the certifications that programs offer. Anyone can offer "certification" and name it what they please. For example, there are several certifications available, each from different organizations, called "Certified Christian Coach." The requirements for each of these "CCC" certifications are different. These certifications may also be referred to as "credentials."

Requirements for various certifications available may include attending classes (the number of hours widely varies), practicing coaching (again, the number of hours required varies widely), mentor coaching or "being coached" (hours and/or duration of time varies), reading and writing assignments, letters of recommendations, and knowledge and skills tests. Some certifications can be obtained by video training and independent study only, while others require significant voice-to-voice instructor contact.

Where coaches from different programs have obtained the ACC, PCC and MCC credentials awarded by the ICF, clear comparisons can be made because these coaches have met the same criteria even though they've taken different classes. However, it is difficult to determine the relative value of certifications or credentials obtained directly from coach training programs for the reasons stated above. ***Certifications or credentials awarded to students by training programs may represent stellar training and excellent proficiency - or they may not.***

Certifications or credentials
awarded to students by training programs
may represent stellar training and excellent proficiency
- or they may not.

SECTION THREE: MAKING THE DECISION THAT'S RIGHT FOR YOU

THE PROCESS

The process for making the decision that's right for you involves prayerfully identifying your mission and vision, and then evaluating the decision-making factors based on your mission and vision.

Step 1: Identify Your Mission and Vision

Step one for making a great decision regarding Christian coach training starts with identifying your calling. Calling is sometimes referred to as "mission" and sometimes as "vision." Just when you think you've got the working definition of those terms down, you will have to think again. "Mission" and "vision" are addressed across a variety of authoritative settings with definitions that are sometimes opposite and sometimes interchangeable, adding up to often times confusing. What school of thought you're from or what training you've taken or what book you've read determines how you use the terms.

I'm inclined to say that your calling is your mission. That is, "calling" or "mission" is what you're going to do. Typically it's a broad statement - contained in a sentence (or so) that includes references to the purpose or significance of your pursuit. Statements of "vision" are longer and more detailed and talk about how things will look when your mission is accomplished.

Whatever you call it, identifying your purpose is the first step. What are you called to? What does God have for you to do? What will it look like when you are living your calling? Before deciding to change your career or invest time and money into training, answer these questions. Start by writing down compelling statements that clearly identify your mission and vision. If you are stymied, this is a great time to work with a trained Christian coach to identify your mission and vision. One place to find a Christian coach is at the free referral service at the Christian Coaches Network website, www.christiancoaches.com.

Why would you start with identifying mission and vision? Why not just "dive in" and "go for it?" Well...because it's important to know where you're going in order to get there!

Consider this quote by Yogi Berra, American baseball player: "If you don't know where you're going, you might wind up someplace else."

Establishing a new career – establishing a new business – is not easy. In your dark hours (and you know they'll come) it helps to know where you're going and why. In those hours you can refer back to your calling - your purpose - the mission and vision statements you've written down - to gain the motivation and courage to press on.

You bought this ebook because you want to make a great choice regarding coach training. You would like to "go somewhere" intentionally.

Then identify your mission and vision. Ask God to show you the vision of where to go. So...write that down.

Step 2 – Evaluate Factors Based on Your Mission and Vision

There are many factors to think through when choosing training. Take a look at your vision (which you have hopefully written down) and identify what will get you there. Will you be coaching in business or ministry? Will you be coaching only Christians? Will you be working in a church or corporate environment? Will you have your own coaching business five or ten years from now?

Each factor you consider and the priority of each factor is determined by your mission and vision. Some of the factors discussed in this book will have little or no importance to you. Very many will. Choose the factors you consider based on the vision God has given you.

Continue to commit your vision and the shaping (and reshaping) of your plans to God in prayer and search scripture for guidance. Tune into the ways that you have received guidance from God in the past – through the godly wisdom of others, personal retreat, prayer journaling, etc. If God leads you to work with a Christian coach, do that.

No one can tell you "the truth about" what training program you should take. That is for you to discover, as you seek God's leading and uncover the unique purposes for which you were created. **God has shown his faithfulness, sustenance and blessing to Christian coaches who have been trained in a variety of programs. God is able to do the same for you as you step into the calling for which you are made.**

Coming next...

Eleven Questions to Ask Yourself When Considering Christian Coach Training

The Factors

1. Ask yourself: Is it coaching or something else?

Is becoming a life coach part of the fulfillment of your true calling? Take a look at your passions and values.

- If you are passionate about helping others heal and resolve personal issues, then *maybe it's not coaching. Maybe it's counseling or therapy.*
- If you love analyzing problems in your field of expertise, summarizing your analysis and making recommendations, then *maybe it's not coaching. Maybe it's consulting.*
- If you deeply desire to help people identify the presence of God in their lives, *then maybe it's not coaching. Maybe it's spiritual direction.*
- Have you looked at the career and ministry options that are similar to coaching and asked yourself which option is truly the best match for your mission?
- Use the Life Coaching Comparison Tool on page 5 to consider the distinctions between coaching and counseling, consulting, spiritual direction, mentoring, discipleship and pastoral care.

Before you commit time and finances to coach training, make sure pursuing coaching will fulfill your mission and vision.

2. Ask yourself: Do I want to be the coach without training?

Once you are sure that coaching is your calling, consider that it is not absolutely required to take training to practice as a coach. Currently no U.S. states require licensing for coaches - so currently there are no "licensing requirements" that can help inform your decision about training. Anyone can decide to be a coach and say so. "Anyone" may not have had coach training of any kind.

So this factor boils down to a question: do you want to be the coach without training? Probably not, since you bought this book. Your vision of your future will reveal whether coach training is necessary to meet your professional or ministry goals. As the author of this Guide I'm not recommending the "no training" path, but I do want to be clear that it is an option.

3. Ask yourself: Is secular coach training an option?

There are many Christian coaches who have trained in secular training programs and this is certainly an option for you, depending on your vision and how God is leading you.

For example, Dr. Gary R. Collins is highly respected as a Christian leader in both the fields of counseling and coaching. As referenced in his book *Christian Coaching: Helping Others Turn Potential into Reality*, Gary took his coach training at the Institute of Life Coach Training (ILCT) - before there was a Christian track at ILCT. In his book he references several other leaders in the Christian coaching field, including Judy Santos, MCC (1942 - 2010), founder of the Christian Coaches Network. Judy took her coach training at Coach U, as did Jane Creswell, MCC. Jane is also a leader in the field and has authored, *Christ-Centered Coaching: Seven Benefits for Ministry Leaders*.

It is entirely possible for Christians to complete training from a secular coach training institution and still retain their Christian faith. Many have done so, though this may not be an easy road to take. As with any training opportunity not taught from a Christian worldview, there can certainly be challenges to Christian faith presented in the training. The term "secular humanism" which is very common in the Christian community, can describe aspects of coach training which are not taught from a Christian worldview. Don't expect or require that your Christian faith will be embraced or celebrated in secular coach training. But if you're prepared to learn coaching skills and practices and don't require this to occur in an openly acknowledged Christian setting, you won't be the first Christian coach that has considered this and gone on to successfully receive excellent coach training while keeping their faith intact.

Only you know where God is leading you, and we know from scripture that God is able to see you through wherever that is.

"I know whom I have believed, and am convinced that he is able to guard what I have entrusted to him for that day." 2 Timothy 1:12b (NIV)

"Now to Him who is able to keep you from stumbling, and to make you stand in the presence of His glory blameless with great joy, to the only God our Savior, through Jesus Christ our Lord, be glory, majesty, dominion and authority, before all time and now and forever. Amen." Jude 24-25 (NASB)

If you are considering coach training options in addition to the Christian programs featured in this Guide, find information at the ICF website (www.coachfederation.org).

4. Ask yourself: Do I want accredited training or not?

Please note: "Accreditation" applies to coach training institutions and programs; "certification" and "credentialing" applies to individual coaches.

Programs are awarded accreditation from the International Coach Federation (ICF). Although ICF has been around the longest, is the largest and currently has the most influence, two other organizations that evaluate coach training have recognition in the professional coaching community. The International Association of Coaches (IAC) licenses schools that meet their standards for professional coach training. And new in 2011, the Center for Credentialing Education approves schools to provide training toward Board Certified Coach (BCC) certification. However, at this time, ICF accreditation is most predominant.

If you take training from an ICF accredited program and follow their prescribed course of action you are steps closer to personally receiving ICF approved credentialing than if you take non-accredited training. At this time, it is possible to obtain ICF credentialling if your training is not ICF accredited by working directly with ICF through a "portfolio" process.

The portfolio application process is described on the ICF website and requires more paperwork and documentation than the application process available to students of ICF accredited training. However, the portfolio process is certainly a feasible option at this time. Part of the portfolio process includes ICF's evaluation of the training under consideration, and the approval granted by ICF is, of course, up to their discretion. Some of the Christian coach training programs profiled in this Guide which are not currently accredited report that students from their programs have successfully used the portfolio process to gain ICF credentialing.

Go to the ICF website (www.coachfederation.org) for a list of accredited programs and information on individual coach credentialing, including options to download applications and all the info necessary to complete the application process.

Keep in mind that anyone can create a training program and award coach certifications. So how do you know that a training program is of the quality you are seeking? How do you know that the certification you would receive holds the value you desire? Well, through the accreditation process, ICF offers structure and standards by which you can evaluate programs and determine the extent to which they meet professional standards. *Programs not accredited by ICF may meet those standards very well, or they may not.*

Also be aware that as training programs apply for ICF accreditation, the process takes time and the outcome is not guaranteed. Perhaps the program you are considering is in the process of applying for accreditation. Be sure to ask - that is, if ICF accreditation and certification is important to you.

ICF awards three types of recognition to training programs - ACTP, ACSTH, and CCE. The following is quoted from the ICF website:

Accredited Coach Training Programs (ACTP)

Each Accredited Coach Training Program (ACTP) offers:

- A minimum of 125 hours of coach-specific training
- Training on all ICF Core Competencies and the ICF Code of Ethics
- A minimum of 6 observed-coaching sessions with an experienced coach
- A comprehensive final exam that evaluates a student's coaching competency

Certified graduates of ACTPs may apply for an ACC or PCC credential using the ACTP graduate application.

Approved Coach Specific Training Hours (ACSTH)

Organizations that offer Approved Coach Specific Training Hours (ACSTH) offer:

- A minimum of 30 hours of coach-specific training
- Training on some ICF Core Competencies and the ICF Code of Ethics
- Students the opportunity to use pre-approved training hours for an ACC, PCC or MCC Portfolio application

Graduates of ACSTH programs applying for an ACC or PCC credential must use the portfolio application rather than the ACTP graduate application. The portfolio application includes an exam.

Continuing Coach Education (CCE)

Continuing Coach Education (CCE) courses further the ongoing development of the professional coach and can be used to satisfy the renewal requirements for credentialed coaches renewing their ACC, PCC, or MCC credentials.

Continuing Coaching Education (CCE) refers to formal courses and seminars that teach skills or tools directly related to ICF Core Competencies, the personal development of the coach, the development of the coach's practice or other skills or tools that are directly applicable to coaching.

Completion of a CCE program alone is generally not enough to satisfy the coach training requirements for a credential.

5. Ask yourself: What type of certification do I want to receive?

Please note: "Certification" and "credentialing" applies to individual coaches; "Accreditation" applies to coach training institutions and programs.

You've probably received SPAM in your email box that announces you can receive a Bachelors Degree or even a PhD with no substantial educational requirements. You are invited to just "call the number," pay the "very reasonable price" and you will be set with letters behind your name. You've probably not taken advantage of this offer.

In the same way you'd want a BA or a PhD to have meaning, you probably want a coach certification with meaning. Deciphering the comparative meanings of the various certifications and credentials offered can be difficult. For help with this, please review the discussion of certifications on page 12.

Two basic types of certification or credentialing exist - certification connected to a professional organization and that which is awarded by a training organization.

Certification by a professional organization, such as ICF or CCN:

ICF certification - *The following is quoted from the ICF website:*

ACC (Associate Certified Coach). The ICF Associate Certified Coach credential is for the practiced coach with at least 100 hours of client coaching experience.

PCC (Professional Certified Coach). The ICF Professional Certified Coach credential is for the proven coach with at least 750 hours of client coaching experience.

MCC (Master Certified Coach). The ICF Master Certified Coach credential is for the expert coach with at least 2,500 hours of client coaching experience.

Christian Coaches Network certification - *The following is quoted from* the CCN Website (www.christiancoaches.com):

CCC (Certified Christian Coach). This credential requires 60 coach specific classroom hours and 100 documented coaching hours, among other requirements.

CPCC (Certified Professional Christian Coach). This credential requires 125 coach specific classroom hours and 750 documented coaching hours, among other requirements.

CMCC (Certified Master Christian Coach). This credential requires 200 coach specific classroom hours and 2,500 documented coaching hours, among other requirements.

Certification through a coach training school:

Many coach training schools offer certifications upon completion of their training programs. The requirements of these certifications vary greatly from school to school. Please refer to page 12 for further discussion of coach training school certifications.

A Masters or D.Min. degree differs from professional certification, but it is certainly an attractive professional distinction. Three schools featured in this book offer graduate degrees with specialization in coaching. Refer to profiles on pages 30-70 for more information.

It is not unusual for a coach to have more than one certification. For example, a coach may have ICF certification, Christian Coaches Network certification and the certification they received through their training school. The value of this is specific to the individual. Some coaches report that their clients are looking for specific certifications. Certifications are "markers" of accomplishment, expertise and credibility, and can provide a sense of personal and professional integrity.

Why is certification important?

Well, increasingly it matters to clients - including churches and ministry organizations. Gary Wood, PCC, president and director of the Christian Coaches Network, has had his eye on the field of Christian coaching since the late '90's. He reports an increase in Christian individuals and organizations looking for coaches with ICF certification.

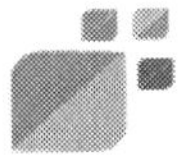

Also, many think that licensing of coaches will become required in the future as the profession matures. So the training decisions you make now could have implications in the future regarding your ease and ability to gain licensing.

If my state doesn't require licensing for coaches, why does certification matter?

Yes, it's true that there are practicing life coaches who have never had professional life coach training. They may be successful in business and they may be good coaches, but - they've never pursued training or ICF certification and they don't plan to.

No, they aren't violating state (USA) regulations at this point. That doesn't mean coaches are free and clear from any possible interest from their state's governing body. In some states coaches have faced challenges - in particular where their work may be perceived as counseling or therapy (just to clarify - *that's not a good thing...*). ICF has information available on these issues. You may also want to check with your local ICF chapter to learn what other professional coaches in your area know about these issues in your state.

> ***The following is helpful information for all Christian coaches to consider.***
>
> Published in the **Journal of Christian Coaching** (Summer 2008), an excerpt from the article entitled *Professional Christian Coaching: How Christian? How Professional?* (page 18) by Christopher McCluskey:
>
> *Although there are some within the Christian coaching community who argue vehemently that we should steer clear of any involvement whatsoever with the established "secular" associations (meaning, primarily, the International Coach Federation - ICF), I am decidedly not of that camp. The truth is that, had it not been for the incredible efforts on the part of hundreds of ICF members and chapters, this profession we are enjoying and beginning to see thrive would already be regulated by the mental health boards in several states! The ICF, and a few other similar associations, have rallied time and again to successfully rebuff aggressive attempts to license coaches in several states. In other words, the only thing standing between our current freedom to practice as professional Christian coaches and regulation of the profession from outside the field has been the often-maligned ICF.*
>
> *An email that has been widely circulated on the web has this to say in response to the above statement: "IF, and I say IF it came to regulation, someone trained as a Christian Life Coach could practice for remuneration the way that Christian counselors now do...by being ordained." WRONG. I'll have to assume the writer of this email is unaware of how many churches have been successfully sued, and often completely shut-down or put into bankruptcy, because of critical errors made in counseling by their ordained counseling staff. Thousands of churches have closed their counseling centers, or forced their counselors to establish professional practices separate from the church, in order to avoid huge liability risks.*

6. Ask yourself: Do I need "niche" or specialized training?

Your vision may include some specifics that can be addressed by specialized training. For example, you may want to specialize in career coaching and offer your services to the niche market of job seekers. Or if you are planning to coach in an international missions or cross-cultural setting, you can possibly benefit from training that is specialized for these applications. There are a variety of niche or specialty training opportunities available. Look for the options as you read the profiles of each training organization found on pages 31-70.

7. Ask yourself: What training logistics are ideal for me?

- Coach training offers many delivery methods. What will work best for you? Over the phone or in person? Group classroom or individual training? Online webinars?
- What location will work for you? Your office? Your deck? Will you travel for training?
- What training schedule will work for you? Number of hours per week? Number of weeks or months? Full days or weekend training?

These are just a few of the logistical options available. Identify the options that best meet your needs as you read the profiles of each training organization found on pages 31-70.

8. Ask yourself: What will I pay for coach training?

As you calculate the costs of coach training, take the following into consideration.

- Start by identifying tuition - the cost of classes.
- Consider the value of what the class offers, *including real time instructor contact training hours.* Real time instructor contact may be in person or voice-to-voice over the phone or via the internet. Put simply, how many hours of voice-to-voice instructor contact are included in the fee you will pay?
- Add up other costs which vary from program to program. For example, added costs can include textbooks, mentor coaching, travel and lodging, website set-up, certification processing, etc.

The estimated costs indicated for each program in the profile section of this book on pages 31-70 are what the training organization has reported to us at the time this Guide was originally prepared. This gives you a picture of comparison at that point in time. You must confirm all costs directly with the training organizations as, of course, these costs change from time to time at the discretion of the training organizations.

9. Ask yourself: What makes a training program excellent?

Quality or excellence is certainly a factor that you want to consider. The following questions can reveal factors in excellence. Each person going through this process of deciding what makes programs excellent will choose different factors and come to different conclusions. Choose the factors of excellence that matter to you.

- How long has the program been around?
- Is the program accredited and by whom?
- What qualifies the faculty to teach coaching?
- Are the instructors successful coaches?
- What coaching credentials do the instructors have?
- How much of the training is voice-to-voice?
- How much of the training is independent or self-directed?
- How does the program define and measure success of grads?
- What support and services does the program offer grads?
- What else matters to you as you assess quality?

Assess many of these factors as you read the profiles of each training organization found on pages 31-70.

10. Ask yourself: How important are Christian coaching community connections?

The community of Christian coaches goes well beyond any one training school. Does it matter to you that your training school acknowledges and supports the greater community of Christian coaches?

I first read the word "co-opetition" in a column by Linda Miller, MCC, published in the Journal of Christian Coaching (Spring 2008, page 18 - now Christian Coaching Magazine). Linda is the co-author (with Chad Hall) of *Coaching for Christian Leaders: A Practical Guide*. In the JOCC article, she describes and calls for a spirit of cooperation, rather than competition, among Christian coaches. She calls this a spirit of "co-opetition."

Does the school you are considering have a spirit of "co-opetition?" Does that matter to you?

Do you believe that Christian coaches, working together and "holding hands" across bridges will be for the good of the Kingdom of God? Do you want your training organization to help facilitate your involvement in the larger Christian community? Then take these thoughts with you as you consider the culture of the training organization you will choose.

"...growing in every way more and more like Christ, who is the head of his body, the church. He makes the whole body fit together perfectly. As each part does its own special work, it helps the other parts grow, so that the whole body is healthy and growing and full of love." Ephesians 4:15-16 (NLT)

11. Ask yourself: Does this program feel like a good match?

It's important not to discount the "good match" factor.

- How does the program "feel" to you? Does it excite you?
- Do you feel confidence in the integrity of the claims in the marketing materials?
- What about the spiritual culture of the program?
- Are you comfortable with or can you accept the spiritual language and expressions used?
- Does the "culture" feel like a place where you can learn?

Ultimately, this may be the factor that you spend the most prayer time on!

Lord, help me be sensitive to your leading as I consider, with you, if this program is the "right fit" for me.

SECTION FOUR:
CHRISTIAN COACH TRAINING PROGRAMS

IDENTIFYING PROGRAMS

To identify programs included in this Guide, two primary methods were used. First, based on the belief that prospective Christian coaches would start on the web, an internet search was conducted to find programs of interest. And secondly, known leaders in the field of Christian coaching were contacted and asked to submit names of programs. The goal was to contact all current Christian coach training programs that train students in classic, professional coaching. Invitations were sent to each of the programs identified.

QUALIFYING PROGRAMS

Once the programs agreed to participate, they were sent information describing the goals of the Guide and asking them to qualify for participation in two main ways. Each program was asked to identify itself as "Christian" and then to acknowledge their alignment with a standard definition of coaching. You can read what was asked of each program on pages 67-73 of this Guide.

Based on the information submitted, all of the programs profiled in this Guide report passionate commitment to identifying themselves as "Christian." As a group, they report that their programs teach coaching from a distinctly Christian worldview. Several of the programs submitted much more information than requested, discussing their use of scripture and demonstrating their integration of Christian faith into the coaching that they teach. Even though some programs submitted more quantity of information regarding their specific

Biblical and theological applications, all report a strong passion and commitment to name Christ as Lord and Savior and to intentionally reflect the teachings of the Bible.

Each program featured in this Guide was also asked to read coaching definitions and a list of key coaching skills and then reply that they were in agreement that their programs were teaching standard professional classic coaching skills. As already noted, each program teaches professional coaching to differing depths. Some programs were specific about reporting additional themes to their coaching curriculum; however each program has acknowledged and reported that the definitions and standards presented are represented in the content of their coach training.

To read the definitions and standards to which each training organization responded, go to pages 80-86 of this Guide.

The next page is a Quick Reference Table that lists all the programs and contact information.

The Complete Guide to Christian Coach Training - Quick Reference

TRAINING ORGANIZATION	WEBSITE	PROGRAM DIRECTOR	CONTACT	CONTACT PHONE
Assembly of God Seminary	http://www.agts.edu/dmin/coaching http://www.agts.edu/macm/coaching	Deborah M. Gill, Ph.D.	Ava Oleson (for D.Min) AOleson@AGTS.edu Randy Walls (for MACM) RWalls@AGTS.edu	417.268.1082 417.268.1045
Center for Coaching Excellence	www.centerforcoachingexcellence.com	Mary Verstraete	Mary Verstraete noelles@centerforcoachingexcellence.com	612.246.4787
Christian Coach Institute	http://www.christiancoachinstitute.com	Janice LaVore-Fletcher	Janice LaVore-Fletcher janice@christiancoachinstitute.com	704.775.3870
Coach Approach Ministries	www.ca-ministries.com	Bill Copper	Bill Copper bcopper@ca-ministries.com	828.256.2126
Coaching4Clergy	http://coaching4clergy.com	J. Val Hastings, MCC	J. Val Hastings, MCC val@coaching4clergy.com	610.385.8034
Coaching Mission International	www.coachingmission.com	Tina Stolzfus Horst	Patty S. MCTcoord@cmiprograms.com	574.534.0400
CoachNet Global LLC	http://coachnet.org	Jonathan Reitz	Judy Pence judy@coachnet.org	888.728.4329
Creative Results Management	www.creativeresultsmanagement.com	Dr. Keith E. Webb, DMin, ACC	Office office@creativeresultsmanagement.com	+1.206.661.81 11
Dream Mentors Transformational Life Coaching Institute	www.dreammentors.org www.dreammentors.biz	Candice Smithyman	Candice Smithyman admin@dreammentors.org	904.272.2266
Erickson College	www.thechristiancoach.com	Marilyn Atkinson	Tony Husted CPC, PCC tony@thechristiancoach.com	206.755.5405
Institute for Life Coach Training	lifecoachtraining.com/index.php/homepage	Dr. Patrick Williams	Ellen Neiley Ritter, Ph.D. ellen@lifecoachtraining.com	888.267.1206
Life Breakthrough Academy	www.lifebreakthroughcoach.com	Daryl and Janet Daughtry	Janet Daughtry training@lifebreakthroughcoach.com	919.576.9098
Life Purpose Coaching Centers International	www.LifePurposeCoachingCenters.com	Katherine Brazelton, PhD, MDiv, MA	Julie Info@LifePurposeCoachingCenters.com	Use Website Contact Form
Lifeforming Leadership Coaching	www.lifeformingcoach.com	Dr. Joseph Umidi	Lyn Eichmann info@lifeformingcoach.com	888.852.2234
Professional Christian Coaching Institute	www.professionalchristiancoaching.com	Christopher McCluskey, PCC	Rachel McCluskey rachel@christian-living.com	573.435.9448
Southwestern Christian University	www.swcu.edu/lifecoaching-institute	John Chasteen	John Chasteen John.chasteen@swcu.edu	405.789.7661 ext 3446
The Academies	www.theacademies.com	Susan Britton Whitcomb, PCC	Lyndsey Lehman, Business Manager Lyndsey@theacademies.com	877.659.3769 ext 4
Way of Life Coaching, LLC	www.wayoflifecoaching.com	Cheryl Scanlan	Cheryl Scanlan Cheryl@wayoflifecoaching.com	919.749.1800
Western Seminary	www.westernseminary.edu	Chad Hall	Lisa Achilles lachilles@westernseminary.edu	503.517.1904
Workplace Coach Institute, Inc. (WCI)	www.workplacecoachinstitute.com	Nancy Branton, MA, PCC	Celeste Kyle celeste@workplacecoachinstitute.com	800.691.2553

Christian Coach Training Program Profiles

The following featured Christian coach training programs provided the information included on their profiles by direct submission to The Complete Guide to Christian Coach Training.

The information on the profiles is subject to change at the discretion of the coach training organizations. This includes certification requirements and the cost of tuition. The reader of the Complete Guide to Christian Coach Training is responsible for verifying all information of interest directly with the training organizations.

Please go to the training organizations' websites and use the phone numbers and contact names provided in the profiles to confirm the information about each program that is key to your decision.

Find the profiles on the following pages:

ASSEMBLIES OF GOD THEOLOGICAL SEMINARY

Website	For D.Min. - http://www.agts.edu/dmin/coaching For MACM - http://www.agts.edu/macm/coaching
Program Director	Deborah M. Gill, Ph.D., Facilitator of AGTS' Professional Coaching Cohorts
Contact Name	For D.Min. - Ava Oleson, D.Min. For MACM - Randy Walls, D.Min.
Contact Email Address	For D.Min. - AOleson@AGTS.edu For MACM - RWalls@AGTS.edu
Contact Phone	For D.Min. - 417.268.1082 For MACM - 417.268.1045
Contact FAX	417.269.1001
Social Media Profiles	
DISTINCTIVES OF ORGANIZATION	The Assemblies of God Theological Seminary offers two accredited academic degrees with a concentration in professional coaching: Master of Arts in Christian Ministries (MACM); and Doctor of Ministry (D.Min.). These programs are delivered in cohorts, as students attend a one-week face-to-face class together on campus in Springfield, MO each semester (fall, spring, and summer). Students receive coach training, observed coaching, and mentor coaching from a variety of experienced Christian coaches and trainers. AGTS programs target the training of Great-Commission professionals to serve Christ within the church and the marketplace. AGTS first offered professional coaching classes in 2010.
Faculty Qualifications	Terminal, academic degrees and coaching certification. Instructional teams are created, partnering a Master Certified Coach instructor with Ph.D. as professor of record, for example.
Accredited by ICF	No
Other Accreditation/Licensing	The seminary has the highest level of accreditation: secular/regional accreditation with the Higher Learning Commission, and seminary accreditation with the Association of Theological Schools.
GRADUATE SCHOOL: PROGRAMS	Doctor of Ministry (D.Min.) OR Master of Arts in Christian Ministry (MACM)
GRADUATE SCHOOL: COURSES	The required academic courses of a seminary education are specially focused on coaching (e.g., Spiritual Life of the Coach, Theological Issues and Contemporary Coaching; Theology of Work; and Ethical Issues and Contemporary Society).

Course Delivery Methods	Students attend one face-to-face class together offered in one-week modules each semester (fall, spring, and summer) in Springfield, MO. Other components of the program are offered through distance learning modes, such as teleconference, videoconference, etc. Between modules, students read and write assignments, receive coaching (mentor coaching and observed coaching evaluations) and practice coaching (peer coaching and client coaching) in fulfillment of class and certification requirements.
GRADUATE SCHOOL: COACHING CERTIFICATION	Depending on the number of client coaching hours they choose to complete between course modules, upon successful completion of the program, students qualify to submit portfolio application to the International Coach Federation as either an Associate Certified Coach or Professional Certified Coach.
GRADUATE SCHOOL: COSTS	The cost of tuition and fees for the Doctor of Ministry (D.Min.) is $17,900 payable in 11 installments of $1,627 over the course of the program. Students pay their own mentor coaches. The cost for the Master of Arts in Christian Ministries (MACM) is approximately $27,000. Tuition and fees are payable the semester each class is taken. Students pay their own mentor coaches.
ADDITIONAL INFORMATION	The coaching courses currently offered at AGTS are only available to the students who are in the AGTS graduate programs. The next MACM Coaching Cohort is scheduled to begin fall of 2012. The D.Min. Coaching Cohort is scheduled to begin spring of 2013. Although this program is not currently accredited by ICF, AGTS has designed its coaching program in consultation with ICF with the intention of creating courses that will align with ICF core competencies and requirements.

The information on these profiles is subject to change at the discretion of the coach training organizations. This includes certification requirements and the cost of tuition. The reader of the Complete Guide to Christian Coach Training is responsible for verifying all information of interest directly with the training organizations.

CENTER FOR COACHING EXCELLENCE

Website	http://www.centerforcoachingexcellence.com
Program Director	Mary Verstraete
Contact Name	Mary Verstraete
Contact Email Address	maryv@centerforcoachingexcellence.com
Contact Phone	612-246-4787
Contact FAX	651-330-8589
Social Media Profiles	
DISTINCTIVES OF ORGANIZATION	A priority for Center for Coaching Excellence (CCE) is to create an environment where trainees experience community. This is achieved by combining face-to-face and telesession training and using the training methodology of *information, application, conversation, and observation©*. Another key distinctive is values-based training. Values are embedded throughout the entire curriculum as trainees study ICF core coaching competencies in-depth.
Faculty Qualifications	130 hours of Coach-Specific Training that meets ICF training requirements and standards; ICF PCC completed; or CCE PCC completed.
Accredited by ICF	No
Other Accreditation/Licensing	No
BASIC COACHING SKILLS PROGRAM	**Professional Coach Training: Essential Coach Training Program**
Year First Student Completed Training	2008
Number of months to complete	3 months
Technology Required	Phone, computer, Internet
BASIC COACHING SKILLS COURSE(S)	**Essential Coach Training**
Training Hours	34.5 hours
Course Delivery Methods	Live Instruction (70%); In-Person (10%); One-on-One (10%); Independent (10%) Two eight hour workshops included in the 12 week course.
BASIC COACHING SKILLS COMPLETION REQUIREMENTS	**Written Assignments; Written Exam; Oral Exam; Buddy/Triad Coaching; Coaching Others; Being Coached**
Coaching Others Hours Required (Client)	6
Being Coached Hours Required (Mentor)	6
Number of Students Who Have Completed Requirements	175
Proprietary Course Materials	Essential Coach Training Manual
Additional Textbooks	Leadership Coaching by Tony Stoltzfus; Co-Active Coaching by Henry Kimsey-House, Karen Kimsey-House, and Phillip Sandahl (third edition)

BASIC COACHING SKILLS CERTIFICATION	Essential Coaching Training Graduate
Additional Certification Requirements	
Additional Certification Costs	
Number of Certifications Awarded	160

BASIC COACHING SKILLS COSTS	
Estimated Cost of basic coaching skills training; includes multiple classes if applicable	$1325
Estimated Cost of Additional Books and Materials	Included
Estimated Cost of Required "Being Coached" hours	$300-$600
Additional Certification Costs	
Other Costs	Travel
Total Cost Estimate	$1625 - 1925 plus travel
Supplemental Cost Explanation	

ADVANCED OR NICHE-SPECIFIC TRAINING	
Advanced or Niche-Specific Training Described	Life Map for Focus Living; Fundamental Coaching Practicum; Mind-Set is Causative; Advanced Coaching Practicum; Ethics, Assessments, Presentation Skills.
ADDITIONAL INFORMATION	CCE offers a We Fly To You program where trainers travel to a city or organization where a group of ten or more trainees will attend the workshops. Workshops are held throughout the US.

The information on these profiles is subject to change at the discretion of the coach training organizations. This includes certification requirements and the cost of tuition. The reader of the Complete Guide to Christian Coach Training is responsible for verifying all information of interest directly with the training organizations.

CHRISTIAN COACH INSTITUTE LLC

Website	http://www.christiancoachinstitute.com
Program Director	Janice LaVore-Fletcher
Contact Name	Janice LaVore-Fletcher
Contact Email Address	Janice@ChristianCoachInstitute.com
Contact Phone	704.926.7037
Contact FAX	877.742.2235
Social Media Profiles	http://twitter.com/coachinstitute http://www.facebook.com/christiancoachinstitute http://ww.linkedin.com/in/christiancoachinstitute http://www.youtube.com/christianlifecoaches
DISTINCTIVES OF ORGANIZATION	Christian Coach Institute integrates several methods of training (weekly group webinars, mentor coach sessions, buddy, coaching lab work, discussion boards and a supportive and encouraging online social community) to deliver a learning experience intended to meet or exceed industry standards for professional coach training. Graduates are prepared to launch a brand new career or they can incorporate their coaching skills into their existing roles.
Faculty Qualifications	Extensive background in Professional Coaching, Licensed Human Behavior Trainer, Adult Learning Techniques, Master Christian Coach Trainer, M.S. Fitness and Adult Wellness, MA Ed., MA Soc.
Accredited by ICF	No
Other Accreditation/Licensing	IAC
BASIC COACHING SKILLS PROGRAM	Certified Christian Life Coach
Year First Student Completed Training	2010
Number of months to complete	4 months
Technology Required	Phone, Computer, Internet
BASIC COACHING SKILLS COURSE(S)	**Certified Christian Life Coach**
Training Hours	32 hours
Course Delivery Methods	Live virtual classroom, i.e. by phone and/or internet - (100%)
BASIC COACHING SKILLS COMPLETION REQUIREMENTS	**Written Assignments; Written Exam; Oral Exam; Buddy/Triad Coaching; Coaching Others; Being Coached**
Coaching Others Hours Required (Client)	8 hours
Being Coached Hours Required (Mentor)	4 hours
Number of Students Who Have Completed Requirements	45
Proprietary Course Materials	Christian Coach Institute Training and Certification Manual

Additional Textbooks	Christian Coaching 2nd Edition by Dr. Gary Collins; Visioneering by Andy Stanley; Get Clients Now by CJ Hayden
BASIC COACHING SKILLS CERTIFICATION	**Certified Christian Life Coach**
Additional Certification Requirements	$150 submitted with application
Additional Certification Costs	
Number of Certifications Awarded	31
BASIC COACHING SKILLS COSTS	
Estimated Cost of basic coaching skills training; includes multiple classes if applicable	$2195
Estimated Cost of Additional Books and Materials	$75
Estimated Cost of Required "Being Coached" hours	Included
Additional Certification Costs	$150
Other Costs	
Total Cost Estimate	$2420
Supplemental Cost Explanation	No Travel Costs
ADVANCED OR NICHE-SPECIFIC TRAINING	
Advanced or Niche-Specific Training Described	Certified Faith and Health Coach; Master Christian Life Coach; Certified Human Behavior Consultant (DISC)
ADDITIONAL INFORMATION	CCI also offers DISC assessments training leading to a designation as a Certified Human Behavior Consultant.

The information on these profiles is subject to change at the discretion of the coach training organizations. This includes certification requirements and the cost of tuition. The reader of the Complete Guide to Christian Coach Training is responsible for verifying all information of interest directly with the training organizations.

COACH APPROACH MINISTRIES

Website	http://www.ca-ministries.com		
Program Director	Bill Copper		
Contact Name	Bill Copper		
Contact Email Address	bcopper@ca-ministries.com		
Contact Phone	828-256-2126		
Contact FAX	828-256-4989		
Social Media Profiles	https://www.facebook.com/pages/Coach-Approach-Ministries/207222329919		
DISTINCTIVES OF ORGANIZATION	Coach Approach Ministries offers a basic certification in Christian leadership coaching, as well as eight additional interactive workshops, each providing 16 hours of training focused on the core competencies of the International Coach Federation. Led by ICF certified instructors and based on Christian coaching philosophy, these courses will help students grow their competencies and develop their skills. Courses are designed to be highly interactive with opportunity for skills practice.		
Faculty Qualifications	ACC certification with demonstrated progress toward PCC.		
Accredited by ICF	No		
Other Accreditation/Licensing	No		
BASIC COACHING SKILLS PROGRAM	**Valwood Christian Leadership Coaching**		
Year First Student Completed Training	2002		
Number of months to complete	4 months		
Technology Required	Computer, Web		
BASIC COACHING SKILLS COURSE(S)	**Intro to Christian Coaching**	**Foundations of Christian Leadership Coaching**	**Establishing a Dynamic Coaching Relationship**
Training Hours	8 hours	16 hours	16 hours
Course Delivery Methods	100% In-Person Training		
BASIC COACHING SKILLS COMPLETION REQUIREMENTS	**Written Assignments, Being Coached**		
Coaching Others Hours Required (Client)			
Being Coached Hours Required (Mentor)	6 hours		
Number of Students Who Have Completed Requirements	900		
Proprietary Course Materials	Onsite courses include Student Manuals, assessments, and videos.		
Additional Textbooks	None required, however a bibliography of recommended reading is provided.		

BASIC COACHING SKILLS CERTIFICATION	Valwood Christian Leadership Coach
Additional Certification Requirements	Valwood Christian Leadership Coaching certification requires 5 steps: Online Intro to Coaching; Onsite Foundations class; Onsite Establishing a Dynamic Coaching Relationship class; Three one-hour teleclasses following the onsite classes; Six hours of Mentor Coaching. In addition, participants are required to engage two persons in a coaching relationship which is monitored by their Mentor Coach.
Additional Certification Costs	N/A
Number of Certifications Awarded	550

BASIC COACHING SKILLS COSTS	
Estimated Cost of basic coaching skills training; includes multiple classes if applicable	$500
Estimated Cost of Additional Books and Materials	
Estimated Cost of Required "Being Coached" hours	
Additional Certification Costs	
Other Costs - meals & lodging	$350
Total Cost Estimate	$900 plus travel
Supplemental Cost Explanation	Cost includes meals and lodging on-site at the Hollifield Leadership Center; add travel costs to Hickory, North Carolina.

ADVANCED OR NICHE-SPECIFIC TRAINING	
Advanced or Niche-Specific Training Described	Coaching Change, Transition and Transformation; Coaching as a Learning Catalyst; The Language of Coaching ; Foundations of Personal Coaching; Coaching Teams; Using Assessment, Inventories, and Tools in Coaching; Launching Your Coaching Practice; and Coach Approach to Evangelism and Discipleship.
ADDITIONAL INFORMATION	Choose from CAM's basic coaching training program (Fast Track) or from the certification program (Valwood Christian Leadership Coaching Certification). CAM s courses are also offered a la carte. In addition to the Hollifield Lesdership Center in Conover, NC, CAM's courses are also taught at NC Tennessee Baptist Center for Coaching, Brentwood, TN.

The information on these profiles is subject to change at the discretion of the coach training organizations. This includes certification requirements and the cost of tuition. The reader of the Complete Guide to Christian Coach Training is responsible for verifying all information of interest directly with the training organizations.

COACHING4CLERGY

Website	http://coaching4clergy.com		
Program Director	J. Val Hastings, MCC		
Contact Name	J. Val Hastings, MCC		
Contact Email Address	val@coaching4clergy.com		
Contact Phone	610.385.8034		
Contact FAX	484.944.1520		
Social Media Profiles	YouTube: http://www.youtube.com/user/jvalhastings Facebook: http://www.facebook.com/coaching4clergy LinkedIn: http://www.linkedin.com/in/valhastings Twitter: http://www.twitter.com/Coaching4Clergy		
DISTINCTIVES OF ORGANIZATION	The Accelerated Coach Training program at Coaching4Clergy is designed to thoroughly equip students to successfully launch a coaching ministry, as well as to apply for their ACC credential through the International Coach Federation. Throughout the training program students observe coaching demonstrations by experienced faculty and mentor-coaches. Every student has multiple opportunities to coach and be coached. A hands-on approach provides participants with core coaching competencies and skill development, which prepares them to use their coaching skills in a variety of settings as both an internal and external coach. This training is chosen by pastors, ministry staff and church leaders. However business and non-profit professionals enroll as well.		
Faculty Qualifications	ICF membership and credential. Successful completion of Coaching4Clergy Trainer and Faculty-in-Training Program. Ongoing participation in monthly faculty development training sessions. Regularly reviewed and evaluated by Coaching4Clergy.		
Accredited by ICF	Coaching4Clergy is accredited by ICF as an ASCTH		
Other Accreditation/Licensing	No		
BASIC COACHING SKILLS PROGRAM	Accelerated Coach Training (64 hours)		
Year First Student Completed Training	2007		
Number of months to complete	6-9 months		
Technology Required	Phone, Computer, Internet		
BASIC COACHING SKILLS COURSE(S)	**Accelerated Coach Training - format one**		**Accelerated Coach Training - format two**
Training Hours	64 hours	**OR**	64 hours
Course Delivery Methods	Live In Person - (60%); Live Virtual Classroom - i.e. by phone and/or internet - (40%)		Live Virtual Classroom - i.e. by phone and/or internet - (100%)
BASIC COACHING SKILLS COMPLETION REQUIREMENTS	**Written Assignments; Written Exam; Oral Exam; Coaching Others; Being Coached**		
Coaching Others Hours Required (Client)	100 hours		
Being Coached Hours Required (Mentor)	10 hours		

Number of Students Who Have Completed Requirements	346
Proprietary Course Materials	The Coaching4Clergy Accelerated Textbook; The Next Great Awakening by J. Val Hastings, MCC; The E-3 Church by J. Val Hastings, MCC
Additional Textbooks	
BASIC COACHING SKILLS CERTIFICATION	**Accelerated Coach Training Certificate**
Additional Certification Requirements	
Additional Certification Costs	
Number of Certifications Awarded	321
BASIC COACHING SKILLS COSTS	
Estimated Cost of basic coaching skills training; includes multiple classes if applicable	$2999
Estimated Cost of Additional Books and Materials	$199
Estimated Cost of Required "Being Coached" hours	$2800 ($400/month for 7 months)
Additional Certification Costs	
Other Costs	$350 (exam fee)
Total Cost Estimate	$6348 (plus possible travel)
Supplemental Cost Explanation	Travel costs may apply based on choice of program.
ADVANCED OR NICHE-SPECIFIC TRAINING	
Advanced or Niche-Specific Training Described	Train-the-Trainer Certification (21 ICF hours); Faculty-in-Training Certification (21 hours); End of Life/Grief Coaching Certification (28 hours)
ADDITIONAL INFORMATION	Coaching4Clergy offers Accelerated Coach Training in two formats: 1-Combination of in-person training (40 hours) and tele-classes (24 hours) OR 2-Total tele-Class (64 hours). The first format is offered in a variety of geographic locations globally. Training locations are posted at the Coaching4Clergy website.

The information on these profiles is subject to change at the discretion of the coach training organizations. This includes certification requirements and the cost of tuition. The reader of the Complete Guide to Christian Coach Training is responsible for verifying all information of interest directly with the training organizations.

COACHING MISSION INTERNATIONAL

Website	http://www.coachingmission.com
Program Director	Tina Stoltzfus Horst
Contact Name	Patty S
Contact Email Address	MCTcoord@cmiprograms.com
Contact Phone	574.534.0400
Contact FAX	
Social Media Profiles	http://www.facebook.com/CoachingMissionInternational
DISTINCTIVES OF ORGANIZATION	CMI's Mission Coach Training program offers professional level coach training for cross-cultural and missions applications. The training is delivered primarily with distance-learning approach comprised of 7 modules over 24 months. One in-person, 5-day set of workshops is also required. Curriculum includes the concepts and practical skills of the core coaching competencies, the conversational coaching model, how to coach life purpose discovery, in addition to the essentials of coaching across cultures and into mission-specific challenges. The core curriculum was developed for CMI by Tony Stoltzfus using open source materials that are available to CMI graduates, enabling them to multiply coaching after graduation within their sphere of influence. CMI provides supervision, one to one coaching and group support to enhance trainee skill development during their first 200 hours of hands-on coaching. Between September 2009 and August 2011, MCT trainees provided over 4387 logged-hours of supervised coaching to more than 446 clients.
Faculty Qualifications	All trainers are professionally trained as coaches and trainers, and have extensive coaching experience, including missions and cross-cultural experience.
Accredited by ICF	No
Other Accreditation/Licensing	
BASIC COACHING SKILLS PROGRAM	Mission Coach Training
Year First Student Completed Training	2011
Number of months to complete	24 months
Technology Required	Phone; computer; web; TV/DVD/CD
BASIC COACHING SKILLS COURSE(S)	**Mission Coach Training - Professional Level**
Training Hours	170 hours
Course Delivery Methods	Live Virtual Classroom Instruction via phone and/or internet (29%); In Person (16%); One on One (8%); Independent (36%); Other (11%). A 5-day in-person set of workshops is required.
BASIC COACHING SKILLS COMPLETION REQUIREMENTS	**Written Assignments; Oral Exam; Buddy/Triad Coaching; Coaching Others; Being Coached**
Coaching Others Hours Required (Client)	200 hours
Being Coached Hours Required (Mentor)	20 hours

Number of Students Who Have Completed Requirements	9
Proprietary Course Materials	Cross Cultural Coaching Workbook, by Tina Stoltzfus. Each Training Module includes custom Trainee packets including assignments and resources: readings, articles, peer practice instructions, and more.
Additional Textbooks	Leadership Coaching;* Leadership Coaching Live CD (set); Coaching Questions; The Christian Life Coaching Handbook; A Leader s Life Purpose Workbook; The Calling Journey; Type Talk, by Otto Kroeger; Ministering Cross-Culturally: An Incarnational Model for Personal Relationships, Sherwood Lingenfelter. *Unless otherwise specified required books are authored by Tony Stoltzfus
BASIC COACHING SKILLS CERTIFICATION	**Graduates are awarded a Professional Coach Training certificate. They may apply for further recognition as a CMI Professional Coach or CMI Master Coach each level with specific training and coaching hours requirements.**
Additional Certification Requirements	
Additional Certification Costs	Included
Number of Certifications Awarded	9
BASIC COACHING SKILLS COSTS	
Estimated Cost of basic coaching skills training; includes multiple classes if applicable	$3245
Estimated Cost of Additional Books and Materials	$150
Estimated Cost of Required "Being Coached" hours	Included
Additional Certification Costs	
Other Costs	travel
Total Cost Estimate	$3395 plus travel
Supplemental Cost Explanation	Travel and lodging related to the set of 5-day in-person workshops are in addition to tuition, books and materials.
ADVANCED OR NICHE-SPECIFIC TRAINING	
Advanced or Niche-Specific Training Described	CMI offers stand-alone, open-to-the-public, teleclasses on specialized coaching areas such as Marriage, Team, Calling Journey, Culture Stress & Re-entry, Conflict, etc.
ADDITIONAL INFORMATION	Current trainers represent 63+ years of missions and cross-cultural experience, including using a coaching orientation in staff and leadership development. Students have the opportunity to participate in an ongoing international, inter-organizational and relationally-oriented community of Cross-cultural Missions Coaches during and after training. Two separate MCT programs are planned for 2012 with onsite workshops conducted in Colorado Springs, Colorado, and India.

The information on these profiles is subject to change at the discretion of the coach training organizations. This includes certification requirements and the cost of tuition. The reader of the Complete Guide to Christian Coach Training is responsible for verifying all information of interest directly with the training organizations.

COACHNET GLOBAL

Website	http://www.coachnet.org	
Program Director	Jonathan Reitz	
Contact Name	Judy Pence	
Contact Email Address	Judy@CoachNet.org	
Contact Phone	1-888-728-4329	
Contact FAX	1-888-728-4329	
Social Media Profiles	http://www.facebook.com/CoachNet http://www.twitter.com/CoachNet http://www.linkedin.com/CoachNet http://www.vimeo.com/CoachNetTV	
DISTINCTIVES OF ORGANIZATION	CoachNet is a multiplication organization that uses coaching as the core skill. CoachNet is established on the belief that coaching is applicable to most any area of life, but specifically focuses on areas that are set up of multiplication. The things done for God's kingdom are the things CoachNet wants to come alongside and help multiply. In addition to training in coaching fundamentals, CoachNet offers advanced coach training and specialized training in key areas that lead to multiplication including coaching for Character, Calling, Competency, and Culture.	
Faculty Qualifications	All CoachNet Faculty have a minimum of 1500 hours of coaching and carry certification from a recognized coach training school. Most have post-graduate degrees in leadership/coaching. All have assessment scores on the CoachNet online assessment in the excellent range.	
Accredited by ICF	No	
Other Accreditation/Licensing		
BASIC COACHING SKILLS PROGRAM	cnStandard (CoachNet Standard Coach Training & Certification)	
Year First Student Completed Training	2004	
Number of months to complete	9 months	
Technology Required	Phone; computer; Internet	
BASIC COACHING SKILLS COURSE(S)	**cnStandard**	**cnStandard for Certification**
Training Hours	16	14
Course Delivery Methods	Live In-Person	
BASIC COACHING SKILLS COMPLETION REQUIREMENTS	**Written Assignments; Written Exam; Buddy/Triad Coaching; Coaching Others; Being Coached**	
Coaching Others Hours Required (Client)	20	
Being Coached Hours Required (Mentor)	10	
Number of Students Who Have Completed Requirements	1200	
Proprietary Course Materials	Coaching 101 by Logan & Carlton; Coaching 101 Handbook by Logan & Reinecke (Author Bob Logan is the founder of CoachNet's program)	

Additional Textbooks	There are several elective options that require additional reading.
BASIC COACHING SKILLS CERTIFICATION	**CoachNet Standard Coach Certification**
Additional Certification Requirements	A portfolio must be submitted and CoachNet's online Assessment score must be 50 or higher for certification.
Additional Certification Costs	
Number of Certifications Awarded	1300+

BASIC COACHING SKILLS COSTS	
Estimated Cost of basic coaching skills training; includes multiple classes if applicable	$2195
Estimated Cost of Additional Books and Materials	
Estimated Cost of Required "Being Coached" hours	
Additional Certification Costs	
Other Costs	
Total Cost Estimate	$2195

Supplemental Cost Explanation	Travel Costs may apply
ADVANCED OR NICHE-SPECIFIC TRAINING	
Advanced or Niche-Specific Training Described	++cnDiscipleship; ++cnLeadership; ++cnAdvanced
ADDITIONAL INFORMATION	CoachNet trains at various locations around the world, mostly in North America. Refer to the website for locations. CoachNet is in partnerships with colleges, universities & seminaries to offer coach training for continuing education units. Call CoacNet for details.

The information on these profiles is subject to change at the discretion of the coach training organizations. This includes certification requirements and the cost of tuition. The reader of the Complete Guide to Christian Coach Training is responsible for verifying all information of interest directly with the training organizations.

CREATIVE RESULTS MANAGEMENT

Website	http://www.creativeresultsmanagement.com
Program Director	Keith E. Webb, DMin, ACC
Contact Name	Office
Contact Email Address	office@crmcoaches.com
Contact Phone	+1.206.661.8111
Contact FAX	
Social Media Profiles	http://www.facebook.com/pages/Creative-Results-Management/337570649732
DISTINCTIVES OF ORGANIZATION	The coach training program at Creative Results Management focuses on integrating Biblical values, ICF core competencies, and a highly interactive and hands-on training style. Ministry leaders from 32 countries have participated, including church planters, missionaries, and those coaching pioneering leaders. Programs are offered in-person at international hub locations in the form of five day intensives followed up by training via phone. The Creative Results Management website doesn't include much Christian language in order to protect the security of participants ministering in limited-access countries. This program is affiliated with Church Resource Ministries (http://www.crmleaders.org), a mission agency specializing in leadership development.
Faculty Qualifications	Faculty are required to meet professional coaching standards, demonstrated by being an ICF certified member. Faculty must meet professional training standards by demonstrating proficiency in Creative Results Management Trainer Competencies and passing an internal train-the-trainer program. Trainers must have extensive ministry experience determined by a behavioral interview.
Accredited by ICF	Approved by ICF for CCE's
Other Accreditation/Licensing	
BASIC COACHING SKILLS PROGRAM	**Core Coaching Skills Certificate Program**
Year First Student Completed Training	2007
Number of months to complete	3 months
Technology Required	Phone
BASIC COACHING SKILLS COURSE(S)	**Core Coaching Skills Certificate Program**
Training Hours	60 hours
Course Delivery Methods	Live Virtual Classroom Instruction, i.e. phone and/or internet (20%); In-Person Instruction (80%)
BASIC COACHING SKILLS COMPLETION REQUIREMENTS	**Written Assignments, Coaching Others**
Coaching Others Hours Required (Client)	25 hours
Being Coached Hours Required (Mentor)	

Number of Students Who Have Completed Requirements	550
Proprietary Course Materials	350-page proprietary manual, including the COACH Model.
Additional Textbooks	
BASIC COACHING SKILLS CERTIFICATION	**Core Coaching Skills Certificate Program Graduate**
Additional Certification Requirements	
Additional Certification Costs	
Number of Certifications Awarded	230
BASIC COACHING SKILLS COSTS	
Estimated Cost of basic coaching skills training; includes multiple classes if applicable	$1445; $995 with early registration
Estimated Cost of Additional Books and Materials	
Estimated Cost of Required "Being Coached" hours	
Additional Certification Costs	
Other Costs	
Total Cost Estimate	$995 - $1445
Supplemental Cost Explanation	Price variation reflects possible early registration discount; Travel costs may apply
ADVANCED OR NICHE-SPECIFIC TRAINING	
Advanced or Niche-Specific Training Described	CRM provides ongoing training and support, including a monthly coach's forum called the Coach's Café, online secure forums, Group Mentor-Coaching for ICF credentialing, and coaching supervision.
ADDITIONAL INFORMATION	In-person training is offered at various locations worldwide. In 2011 training was offered Seattle, Denver, Annapolis MD, Singapore, London, Spain, and China. CRM has collected data to show that some graduates have received their ICF ACC credential via the portfolio application using only CRM's training hours. CRM's trainers are qualified to provide ICF mentor-coaching and coaching supervision. Three CRM trainers serve on ICF chapter board of directors.

The information on these profiles is subject to change at the discretion of the coach training organizations. This includes certification requirements and the cost of tuition. The reader of the Complete Guide to Christian Coach Training is responsible for verifying all information of interest directly with the training organizations.

DREAM MENTORS INTERNATIONAL

Website	http://www.dreammentors.org		
Program Director	Dr. Candice Smithyman		
Contact Name	Dr. Candice Smithyman		
Contact Email Address	Candice@dreammentors.org		
Contact Phone	904-318-8811		
Contact FAX	904-272-2266		
Social Media Profiles			
DISTINCTIVES OF ORGANIZATION	The Dream Mentors Transformational Life Coaching Institute provides training in the area of biblical life coaching and transformational life coaching. Classes integrate coaching skills competencies with God's Word. The curriculum includes visual diagrams and life coaching strategies to use with clients. Two types of programs are offered: certificate of completion and credentialing.		
Faculty Qualifications	Masters in Counseling, Psychology, Theology		
Accredited by ICF	No		
Other Accreditation/Licensing	ACSI: Association of Christian Schools International for Continuing Education Credits		
BASIC COACHING SKILLS PROGRAM	Basic Biblical Life Coaching Program		
Year First Student Completed Training	2009		
Number of months to complete	3 months		
Technology Required	Phone, Computer, Internet		
BASIC COACHING SKILLS COURSE(S)	**Basic Biblical Life Coaching Certificate of Completion**	**OR**	**Associate Biblical Life Coach Credential**
Training Hours	30		50
Course Delivery Methods	Self-paced/student-directed/independent study (100%)		Live Virtual Classroom Instruction - i.e. Phone and/or internet (40%); Self-paced/ student-directed/independent study (60%).
BASIC COACHING SKILLS COMPLETION REQUIREMENTS	**Written Exam; Coaching Others; Being Coached**		
Coaching Others Hours Required (Client)	75		
Being Coached Hours Required (Mentor)	20		
Number of Students Who Have Completed Requirements	60		
Proprietary Course Materials	Audio mp3 files, power points, books		

Additional Textbooks	Christian Coaching (2001) by Dr. Gary Collins; Spiritual Direction and Meditation (1960) by Thomas Merton; Coaching for Christian Leaders (2007) by Linda Miller and Chad Hall; Coaching Questions: A Coaches Guide to Powerful Asking Skills (2008) by Tony Stoltzfus; Celebration of Discipline (1988) by Richard Foster
BASIC COACHING SKILLS CERTIFICATION	**The certificate of completion is awarded with demonstration of completing the online self-study training and a written exam. For the Associate Biblical Life Coach credential, 20 additional voice-to-voice training hours with a mentor coach is required.**
Additional Certification Requirements	
Additional Certification Costs	$35 administrative fee if you would like a paper copy of your credential mailed to you online certificate is free or $35 admin fee for paper certificate
Number of Certifications Awarded	60

BASIC COACHING SKILLS COSTS	
Estimated Cost of basic coaching skills training; includes multiple classes if applicable	Free (for 30 hours) or $250 for additional 20 hours of voice-to-voice training
Estimated Cost of Additional Books and Materials	$100-$200
Estimated Cost of Required "Being Coached" hours	
Additional Certification Costs	
Other Costs	
Total Cost Estimate	$0 - $485
Supplemental Cost Explanation	depending the student's choice of certificate or credential

ADVANCED OR NICHE-SPECIFIC TRAINING	
Advanced or Niche-Specific Training Described	Advanced Transformational Life Coach is offered along with a Professional Biblical Life Coaching credential
ADDITIONAL INFORMATION	Dream Mentors Transformational Life Coaching motto is to "BE a coach, Don't just DO Coaching," which is intended to focus on transforming students by teaching them strategies that enable them to experience transformation first through advancing their relationship with Jesus Christ. In-person training can be arranged in Orange Park, FL. Dream Mentors International is affiliated with the International Tribune of Christian Coaches (ITCC).

The information on these profiles is subject to change at the discretion of the coach training organizations. This includes certification requirements and the cost of tuition. The reader of the Complete Guide to Christian Coach Training is responsible for verifying all information of interest directly with the training organizations.

ERICKSON COLLEGE INTERNATIONAL

Website	http://www.thechristiancoach.com
Program Director	Marilyn Atkinson
Contact Name	Tony Husted
Contact Email Address	tony@thechristiancoach.com
Contact Phone	206-755-5405
Contact FAX	
Social Media Profiles	
DISTINCTIVES OF ORGANIZATION	The Erickson College program is the first (and at the release of this ebook, the only) ICF ACTP program taught entirely to a Christian audience, with Christian content, by a Christian trainer from start to finish. The Art and Science of Coaching offers the skills, questions, and strategies to coach both believers and non-believers. The Art and Science of coaching: A Transformational Christian Program is a unique course designed for professionals, pastoral and lay persons who want to assist others in developing their own God given talents, strengths, gifts, and vision. The course is taught from a Judeo-Christian worldview, taking into account the ministry of the Holy Spirit, Biblical Truth and God's Redemptive Plan.
Faculty Qualifications	ICF PCC, Graduate of the Program Completion of 8 Day Trainer's Training, Successful Coaching Practice for a minimum of 1 year, 1 year training apprenticeship
Accredited by ICF	Accredited by ICF as an ACTP
Other Accreditation/Licensing	
BASIC COACHING SKILLS PROGRAM	The Art and Science of Coaching
Year First Student Completed Training	2001
Number of months to complete	10 months
Technology Required	Internet
BASIC COACHING SKILLS COURSE(S)	**The Art and Science of Coaching**
Training Hours	125 hours
Course Delivery Methods	Live Virtual Classroom Instruction, i.e. phone and/or internet (100%)
BASIC COACHING SKILLS COMPLETION REQUIREMENTS	**Written Exam, Coaching Others, Other**
Coaching Others Hours Required (Client)	25
Being Coached Hours Required (Mentor)	
Number of Students Who Have Completed Requirements	150
Proprietary Course Materials	400 Page proprietary Manual

Additional Textbooks		
BASIC COACHING SKILLS CERTIFICATION	**Erickson Professional Coach**	
Additional Certification Requirements		
Additional Certification Costs		
Number of Certifications Awarded	100+	
BASIC COACHING SKILLS COSTS		
Estimated Cost of basic coaching skills training; includes multiple classes if applicable		$4600
Estimated Cost of Additional Books and Materials		
Estimated Cost of Required "Being Coached" hours		
Additional Certification Costs		
Other Costs		
Total Cost Estimate		$4600
Supplemental Cost Explanation		
ADVANCED OR NICHE-SPECIFIC TRAINING		
Advanced or Niche-Specific Training Described	ACTP Testing, Team Coaching, NLP Practitioner and Master Practitioner, Family Coaching, Trainers Training.	
ADDITIONAL INFORMATION	As the information above demonstrates, the Erickson student purchases the entire program at one price - from basic coach training through advanced training that is altogether ACTP accredited by ICF.	

The information on these profiles is subject to change at the discretion of the coach training organizations. This includes certification requirements and the cost of tuition. The reader of the Complete Guide to Christian Coach Training is responsible for verifying all information of interest directly with the training organizations.

INSTITUTE FOR LIFE COACH TRAINING

Website	http://lifecoachtraining.com/index.php/homepage
Program Director	Dr. Patrick Williams
Contact Name	Ellen Neiley Ritter, Ph.D.
Contact Email Address	ellen@lifecoachtraining.com
Contact Phone	888.267.1206
Contact FAX	
Social Media Profiles	http://www.facebook.com/#!/pages/Institute-for-Life-Coach-Training/338510102544
DISTINCTIVES OF ORGANIZATION	The Institute for Life Coach Training (ILCT) offers the first professional coach training program accredited by the International Coach Federation. ILCT offers a coach training program providing the tools for reaching and empowering clients who are seeking to grow in the context of their Christian faith, inspiring growth in accordance with one's God given gifts and talents.
Faculty Qualifications	All ILCT faculty are professionally credentialed coaches and that majority also hold an advanced degree in the helping professions.
Accredited by ICF	Accredited by ICF as ACTP*
Other Accreditation/Licensing	This program is approved by The Center for Credentialing Education (CCE) towards their Board Certified Coach (BCC) credential. Approved under the MyCAA program under Military One Source. Approved for providing CEU's by the National Board of Certified Counselors and the National Association of Alcohol and Addiction Counselors.
BASIC COACHING SKILLS PROGRAM	**Amplified Foundational Course for Christian Coaches**
Year First Student Completed Training	2001
Number of months to complete	5 months
Technology Required	Phone; Web
BASIC COACHING SKILLS COURSE(S)	**Amplified Foundational Course for Christian Coaches**
Training Hours	40 hours
Course Delivery Methods	Live virtual classroom instruction (i.e. via live webinar/phone) 100%
BASIC COACHING SKILLS COMPLETION REQUIREMENTS	**Written or Computer-based Exam; Buddy/Triad Coaching**
Coaching Others Hours Required (Client)	
Being Coached Hours Required (Mentor)	
Number of Students Who Have Completed Requirements	

Proprietary Course Materials	Students in the course are provided with two manuals, included in the cost for the course. 1) The ILCT Foundational Guidebook, which provides materials to increase growth as a masterful coach. 2) The Amplified Christian manual, which identifies relevant passages from the scriptures which relate to each of the lessons, address the coach's growth, and apply to the coaching process.
Additional Textbooks	Becoming a Professional Life Coach: Lessons from the Institute for Life Coach Training By Dr. Patrick Williams, Founder of ILCT
BASIC COACHING SKILLS CERTIFICATION	**Completion of all requirements of the Amplified Foundational Course for Christian Coaches will result in students being awarded a certificate identifying them as a Graduate of the ILCT Amplified Foundational Course for Christian Coaches.**
Additional Certification Requirements	
Additional Certification Costs	
Number of Certifications Awarded	Approximately 600

BASIC COACHING SKILLS COSTS	
Estimated Cost of basic coaching skills training; includes multiple classes if applicable	$2295
Estimated Cost of Additional Books and Materials	
Estimated Cost of Required "Being Coached" hours	
Additional Certification Costs	
Other Costs	$25
Total Cost Estimate	$2320

Supplemental Cost Explanation	No travel costs
ADVANCED OR NICHE-SPECIFIC TRAINING	
Advanced or Niche-Specific Training Offered	Yes
Advanced or Niche-Specific Training Described	As an ICF Accredited Coach Training Program, ILCT offers a full program which will qualify you to become credentialed as an ACC or a PCC. ILCT also has a number of certification programs available including certification as a Certified Life Coach, as a Business Coaching Specialist, a Relationship Coaching Specialist, and as a Wellness Coaching Specialist.
ADDITIONAL INFORMATION	*Students who take The Amplified Foundational Course for Christian Coaches at ILCT can choose other courses that combined are accredited by ICF as an ACTP. Not all of the other combined courses are taught from a distinctly Christian perspective. The initial course is offered a la carte. However, some Christian students who have started with the Foundational course have chosen to continue their classes with ILCT and complete this ACTP. For information specifically on The Amplified Foundational Course for Christian Coaches at ILCT, follow this link: http://lifecoachtraining.com/index.php/programs/all_courses/the_foundational_course_for_christian_coaches/

The information on these profiles is subject to change at the discretion of the coach training organizations. This includes certification requirements and the cost of tuition. The reader of the Complete Guide to Christian Coach Training is responsible for verifying all information of interest directly with the training organizations.

LIFE BREAKTHROUGH ACADEMY

Website	www.lifebreakthroughcoach.com
Program Director	Daryl Daughtry
Contact Name	Janet Daughtry
Contact Email Address	training@lifebreakthroughcoach.com
Contact Phone	919-926-9647
Contact FAX	
Social Media Profiles	Facebook: http://www.facebook.com/lifebreakthrough Twitter: http://www.twitter.com/lifebreakthru
DISTINCTIVES OF ORGANIZATION	In addition to industry-standard coaching skills and competencies, Life Breakthrough Academy focuses on Biblical identity, core values, life purpose, healthy mindset, and goals achievement.
Faculty Qualifications	Trained, certified, experienced in life coaching, Biblically literate, and a gifted trainer. Trainers have completed the Life Breakthrough Academy course and have received this certification as well as other credentials.
Accredited by ICF	No
Other Accreditation/Licensing	
BASIC COACHING SKILLS PROGRAM	**Life Breakthrough Coaching**
Year First Student Completed Training	2009
Number of months to complete	3 months
Technology Required	Phone, computer, internet
BASIC COACHING SKILLS COURSE(S)	**Certified Life Breakthrough Coach**
Training Hours	30 hours
Course Delivery Methods	Live Virtual Classroom Instruction, i.e. via phone and/or internet (33%); Self-paced/student-directed/independent study (67%)
BASIC COACHING SKILLS COMPLETION REQUIREMENTS	**Written Assignments; Written Exam; Buddy/Triad Coaching; Coaching Others; Other**
Coaching Others Hours Required (Client)	
Being Coached Hours Required (Mentor)	
Number of Students Who Have Completed Requirements	203
Proprietary Course Materials	Written assignments and worksheets, written exam, practice-coaching written dialogues, Buddy coach coaching, and live coaching others.

Additional Textbooks	"Christian Coaching" (2nd Edition) by Dr. Gary R. Collins; "The Lies We Believe" by Dr. Chris Thurman; "Powerful Questions" by Tony Stoltzfus (optional); and "Co-Active Coaching" by Laura Whitworth (optional).
BASIC COACHING SKILLS CERTIFICATION	**Certified Life Breakthrough Coach or Certified Biblical Life Coach**
Additional Certification Requirements	Must verbally participate in class and exhibit an understanding of coaching skills and techniques. Must exhibit personal and spiritual maturity.
Additional Certification Costs	
Number of Certifications Awarded	161
BASIC COACHING SKILLS COSTS	
Estimated Cost of basic coaching skills training; includes multiple classes if applicable	$699
Estimated Cost of Additional Books and Materials	$35
Estimated Cost of Required "Being Coached" hours	
Additional Certification Costs	
Other Costs	
Total Cost Estimate	$734
Supplemental Cost Explanation	An option for Solo training adds $198 to the total cost
ADVANCED OR NICHE-SPECIFIC TRAINING	
Advanced or Niche-Specific Training Described	We offer coach mentoring, leadership coach training and marketing training.
ADDITIONAL INFORMATION	Life Breakthrough Academy's describes their training as competency-based and breakthrough-based, as well as formational and transformational. Life Breakthrough Academy is affiliated with the Biblical Coaching Alliance.

The information on these profiles is subject to change at the discretion of the coach training organizations. This includes certification requirements and the cost of tuition. The reader of the Complete Guide to Christian Coach Training is responsible for verifying all information of interest directly with the training organizations.

LIFE PURPOSE COACHING CENTERS INTERNATIONAL®

Website	www.LifePurposeCoachingCenters.com		
Program Director	Katherine Brazelton, PhD, MDiv, MA		
Contact Name	Julie		
Contact Email Address	info@LifePurposeCoachingCenters.com		
Contact Phone	Use Email for initial contact		
Contact FAX			
Social Media Profiles	http://www.facebook.com/katie.brazelton http://twitter.com/KatieBrazelton http://www.linkedin.com/in/katiebrazelton http://www.pathwaytopurpose.blogspot.com http://www.charactermakeoverblog.blogspot.com http://katiebrazelton.myplaxo.com		
DISTINCTIVES OF ORGANIZATION	Life Purpose Coaching Centers International® teaches coaching from a "life purpose" focus which puts all client goals, actions, steps, stumbling blocks, fears, motives, passions, dreams, testimony, health, finances, career, relationships, etc., into perspective - according to God's unique master plan for fulfillment and significance. LPCCI is the only training organization to teach Katie Brazelton's proprietary products including Life Purpose Coach® 2-Day Intensive Breakthrough Facilitation process, a 20-minute LaserCoaching(SM) process for individuals, a standard 50-minute coaching sessions (proprietary process), and an advanced 1-day intensive coaching processes for couples and young adults.		
Faculty Qualifications	Terminal Degree such as PhD, PsyD, DMin, or JD and extensive field experience.		
Accredited by ICF	Approved by ICF for CCE's		
Other Accreditation/Licensing	Certified to offer CEU's through the IACET (International Association of Continuing Education Training)		
BASIC COACHING SKILLS PROGRAM	**LIFE PURPOSE COACH®**		
Year First Student Completed Training	2006		
Number of months to complete	6-12 months		
Technology Required	Phone, computer, web		
BASIC COACHING SKILLS COURSE(S)	**Life Purpose Coach®**	**Setting Up and Marketing Your Life Purpose Coach Business**	**Life Purpose Coach 2-Day Breakthrough Facilitation**
Training Hours	17 hour	14 hours	22 hours
Course Delivery Methods	Live Virtual Classroom (25%) One-to-One (25%) Independent (50%)	Live Virtual Classroom (25%) One-to-One (10%) Independent (60%)	Live (50%) One-to-One (20%) Independent (30%
BASIC COACHING SKILLS COMPLETION REQUIREMENTS	**Written Assignments; Written Exam; Buddy/Triad Coaching; Coaching Others; Being Coached**		
Coaching Others Hours Required (Client)	23		
Being Coached Hours Required (Mentor)	23		

Number of Students Who Have Completed Requirements	450
Proprietary Course Materials	For each class, 5-10 proprietary, 30-page, E-Workbooks; Client's Electronic Templates, such as Conversation EZ-Forms and Your Life on the Movie Screen® by Brazelton
Additional Textbooks	Pathway to Purpose for Women by Brazelton; The Power of a Loving Man by Jernigan; Conversations on Purpose by Brazelton; Your Spiritual Gifts by Wagner; Character Makeover: 40 Days with a Life Coach to Create the Best You by Brazelton/Leith; Live Big by Brazelton; Purpose Driven Life by Warren: SHAPE by Rees; Praying for Purpose for Women by Brazelton; Living the Life You Were Meant to Live by Patterson
BASIC COACHING SKILLS CERTIFICATION	**After 101 and 201, graduate receives the LPC-Associate Certification. After 301, graduate receives LPC-Professional Certification.**
Additional Certification Requirements	None
Additional Certification Costs	$125 for LPCCI Landing Page link for World MAP
Number of Certifications Awarded	325

BASIC COACHING SKILLS COSTS	
Estimated Cost of basic coaching skills training; includes multiple classes if applicable	$3200
Estimated Cost of Additional Books and Materials	$100
Estimated Cost of Required "Being Coached" hours	$250
Additional Certification Costs	$125
Other Costs	
Total Cost Estimate	$3675

Supplemental Cost Explanation	
ADVANCED OR NICHE-SPECIFIC TRAINING	
Advanced or Niche-Specific Training Described	Advanced Coach Training: Elective courses are offered in Course 401a-b-c-d-e to teach strategic coach facilitation processes, such as: couples, young adults, grief, divorce, and LaserCoaching(SM).
ADDITIONAL INFORMATION	Life Purpose Coach® students learn to use LPCCI's proprietary, marquee coaching process, Your Life on the Movie Screen®. Utilizing this modern-techno Electronic Template, a client's life flashes up on a 22-50 inch LCD viewing screen for two days (8am-5pm), with him/her receiving the coaching documents printed out upon completion. Program developer, Dr. Katie Brazelton, is a bestselling author of eight books. She is also an Inaugural Board Member of International Christian Coaching Association (ICCA). Onsite training is scheduled periodically in locations such as Laguna Beach, CA; Kauai/Maui; Switzerland/France; and South Africa.

The information on these profiles is subject to change at the discretion of the coach training organizations. This includes certification requirements and the cost of tuition. The reader of the Complete Guide to Christian Coach Training is responsible for verifying all information of interest directly with the training organizations.

LIFEFORMING LEADERSHIP COACHING

Website	http://www.lifeformingcoach.com		
Program Director	Dr. Joseph Umidi		
Contact Name	Lyn Eichmann		
Contact Email Address	info@lifeformingcoach.com		
Contact Phone	888-852-2234		
Contact FAX			
Social Media Profiles			
DISTINCTIVES OF ORGANIZATION	Within their vocational field, Lifeforming trains coaches to coach leaders and influence lives through a transformational coaching relationship. Lifeforming uses both ICF competencies and ethics, combined with biblical values to develop coaches to impact nations. Coach training centers are located nationally and internationally. Lifeforming curriculum is also taught in classes through Regent University, Southwest Christian University and Canyon Hills Bible College for academic credit.		
Faculty Qualifications	ICF level of coach training hours, ICF level of paid coaching hours, Masters or Doctoral degrees for academic credit applied to coach training program		
Accredited by ICF	No		
Other Accreditation/Licensing	No		
BASIC COACHING SKILLS PROGRAM	Accelerated Coach Training OR Formation Track		
Year First Student Completed Training	2000		
Number of months to complete	3.5 months		
Technology Required	Phone; Computer, Internet		
BASIC COACHING SKILLS COURSE(S)	**Accelerated Coach Training**		**Formation Track**
Training Hours	55 hours	**OR**	55 hours
Course Delivery Methods	Live Virtual Classroom Instruction: 15% In Person: 30% One to One: 10% Independent: 30% Other 15%		Live Virtual Classroom Instruction: 34 % One to One: 16% Independent: 30% Other 20%
BASIC COACHING SKILLS COMPLETION REQUIREMENTS	**Written Assignments; Oral Exam; Buddy/Triad Coaching; Coaching Others; Being Coached**		
Coaching Others Hours Required (Client)	4		
Being Coached Hours Required (Mentor)	6		
Number of Students Who Have Completed Requirements	3219		
Proprietary Course Materials	ACT Accelerated Coach Training Manual, Lifeforming Leadership Coaching Formation Coaching Manual, available in multiple languages.		

Additional Textbooks	
BASIC COACHING SKILLS CERTIFICATION	**Lifeforming Growth Coach Certificate**
Additional Certification Requirements	
Additional Certification Costs	
Number of Certifications Awarded	3058

BASIC COACHING SKILLS COSTS	
Estimated Cost of basic coaching skills training; includes multiple classes if applicable	$1016.45
Estimated Cost of Additional Books and Materials	
Estimated Cost of Required "Being Coached" hours	
Additional Certification Costs	
Other Costs	
Total Cost Estimate	$1016.45

Supplemental Cost Explanation	There may be additional expense for travel.
ADVANCED OR NICHE-SPECIFIC TRAINING	
Advanced or Niche-Specific Training Described	The Life Focus Track provides 56 coach training hours in destiny discovery and goal setting skills. The Implementation Track provides 63 coach training hours in higher level coaching skills, techniques and supervised coaching. Lifeforming also has several niche specific, 8-week online programs, including uniquely designed assessments and an introduction to coaching skills
ADDITIONAL INFORMATION	In-person training is offered in Virginia Beach, VA, as well as training locations in CA, OK, GA, NJ, FL, Italy, Philippines, El Salvador, UK, South Africa, France, Norway, Singapore, Kenya. In some training situations, we will bring training to the site of an organization.

PROFESSIONAL CHRISTIAN COACHING INSTITUTE

Website	www.ProfessionalChristianCoaching.com
Program Director	Christopher McCluskey, PCC, CMCC
Contact Name	Rachel McCluskey, Director of Admissions
Contact Email Address	rachel@christian-living.com
Contact Phone	(573) 435-9448
Contact FAX	(573) 435-9538
Social Media Profiles	http://www.facebook.com/ChristianLifeCoachTraining http://twitter.com/#!/pccicoaching http://www.linkedin.com/company/professional-christian-coaching-institute http://www.youtube.com/user/ChristianCoaching
DISTINCTIVES OF ORGANIZATION	Professional Christian Coaching Institute (PCCI) offers a complete program of training in professional-grade coaching in alignment with the standards of the International Coach Federation (ICF). The program integrates three core principles: Solid Christian Faith, Strong Coaching Competencies, and Solid Business Practices. Training at PCCI takes a whole-person approach, addressing physical, mental, emotional, relational & spiritual issues from an ontological ('being') as well as a practical ('doing') perspective. Students are equipped in the mindset, skills, tools & techniques of effective coaching.
Faculty Qualifications	Coaches with established coaching businesses who are certified by the International Coach Federation (ICF) at either the ACC, PCC or MCC levels.
Accredited by ICF	No
Other Accreditation/Licensing	
BASIC COACHING SKILLS PROGRAM	**The Essentials of Coaching**
Year First Student Completed Training	2010
Number of months to complete	4 months
Technology Required	Phone; Computer; Internet
BASIC COACHING SKILLS COURSE(S)	**The Essentials of Coaching**
Training Hours	30 hours
Course Delivery Methods	Live virtual classroom Instruction, i.e. via phone and/or internet (100%)
BASIC COACHING SKILLS COMPLETION REQUIREMENTS	**Written Assignments; Buddy/Triad Coaching; Other**
Coaching Others Hours Required (Client)	
Being Coached Hours Required (Mentor)	
Number of Students Who Have Completed Requirements	102

Proprietary Course Materials	DVD/CD entitled "A Crash Course in Christian Coaching" by Christopher McCluskey, PCC, CMCC; Proprietary curriculum guide
Additional Textbooks	"Christian Coaching" by Dr. Gary Collins; "Co-Active Coaching" by Laura Whitworth et al; "Becoming a Professional Life Coach" by Dr. Patrick Williams.
BASIC COACHING SKILLS CERTIFICATION	**Students receive a Certificate of Completion for The Essentials of Coaching and receive a Certified Professional Life Coach designation with additional requirements**
Additional Certification Requirements	The Certified Professional Life Coach (CPLC) is awarded to those who complete The Essentials of Coaching class along with two supervised practicums (Coaching Skills Development & Coaching Skills Mastery), and a 6-hour course entitled Ethical Practice and Liability Risk Management. CPLCs are also required to have provided at least 50 hours of professional coaching to clients and to have had at least 5 hours of private mentor coaching themselves.
Additional Certification Costs	None
Number of Certifications Awarded	13 (new in 2011)

BASIC COACHING SKILLS COSTS	
Estimated Cost of basic coaching skills training; includes multiple classes if applicable	$1800
Estimated Cost of Additional Books and Materials	$65
Estimated Cost of Required "Being Coached" hours	N/A
Additional Certification Costs	N/A
Other Costs	
Total Cost Estimate	$1865

Supplemental Cost Explanation	No travel costs
ADVANCED OR NICHE-SPECIFIC TRAINING	
Advanced or Niche-Specific Training Described	Advanced: "Coaching Skills Development" (20 hours), "Coaching Skills Mastery" (20 hours), and "Ethical Practice & Liability Risk Management in Coaching" (6 hours). Specialty or niche-specific courses: The Accidental Entrepreneur," "Group Coaching", "Leadership Coaching," "Effective Marketing in the 21st Century", "Career Coaching", and "Coaching for Spiritual Formation".
ADDITIONAL INFORMATION	This program is developed by Christopher McCluskey, a pioneer in Christian coaching and founder of the first Christian training program to be accredited by the ICF in 2003. The core faculty at PCCI have more than eleven years of experience delivering coach training more than 1000 students worldwide.

The information on these profiles is subject to change at the discretion of the coach training organizations. This includes certification requirements and the cost of tuition. The reader of the Complete Guide to Christian Coach Training is responsible for verifying all information of interest directly with the training organizations.

SOUTHWESTERN CHRISTIAN UNIVERSITY LIFECOACHING INSTITUTE

Website	http://www.swcu.edu/lifecoaching-institute		
Program Director	John Chasteen		
Contact Name	John Chasteen		
Contact Email Address	John.chasteen@swcu.edu		
Contact Phone	405-789-7661 ext. 3446		
Contact FAX	405-495-7800		
Social Media Profiles	www.facebook.com/SCULifecoachingInstitute www.twitter/sculci www.heycoachjohn.com		
DISTINCTIVES OF ORGANIZATION	**Southwestern Christian University's LifeCoaching Institute offers coach training for various levels of certification both in conjuction with the degree program and available to those not desiring a degree. A fully accredited Master of Ministry degree in Life coaching is available.**		
Faculty Qualifications	Coaching faculty are certified trainers with LifeForming Leadership Coaching of Virginia Beach, VA.		
Accredited by ICF	No		
Other Accreditation/Licensing	SWCU is academically accredited with the North Central Higher Learning Commission.		
BASIC COACHING SKILLS PROGRAM	**The following training is offered to students not pursuing a graduate degree.**		
Year First Student Completed Training	2007		
Number of months to complete	12 months - each module takes 15 weeks to complete		
Technology Required	Phone -		
BASIC COACHING SKILLS COURSE(S)	**Life Coaching - Formation**	**Life Coaching - Life Focus**	**Life Coaching - Implementation**
Training Hours	54 hours	54 hours	54 hours
Course Delivery Methods	One-on-One (35%); Independent (40%); Other (25%) Other: 1.5 day in person workshop - On campus at Bethany OK, and at our Tulsa Metro site		
BASIC COACHING SKILLS COMPLETION REQUIREMENTS	**Written Assignments; Oral Exam; Buddy/Triad Coaching; Coaching Others**		
Coaching Others Hours Required (Client)	8		
Being Coached Hours Required (Mentor)			
Number of Students Who Have Completed Requirements	60+		
Proprietary Course Materials			

Additional Textbooks	
BASIC COACHING SKILLS CERTIFICATION	**LifeForming Leadership Coach**
Additional Certification Requirements	
Additional Certification Costs	
Number of Certifications Awarded	100+

BASIC COACHING SKILLS COSTS	
Estimated Cost of basic coaching skills training; includes multiple classes if applicable	$3300
Estimated Cost of Additional Books and Materials	$50
Estimated Cost of Required "Being Coached" hours	
Additional Certification Costs	
Other Costs	
Total Cost Estimate	$3350

Supplemental Cost Explanation	Additional travel costs may apply
ADVANCED OR NICHE-SPECIFIC TRAINING	
Advanced or Niche-Specific Training Offered	Yes - see Graduate School Information below.
GRAD SCHOOL INFORMATION	In addition to the coach training above, (offered to non-degree students), SWCU offers a graduate degree - Master of Ministry in Life coaching, a 36 hour program. Find more on the Master of Ministry in Life Coaching at this link: http://www.swcu.edu/lifecoaching-institute The graduate program is live training, delivered on site at two campuses, Bethany, OK and Tulsa, OK.
ADDITIONAL INFORMATION	Coaching as a Career class is offered to help the student set up their coaching business and target their market.

The information on these profiles is subject to change at the discretion of the coach training organizations. This includes certification requirements and the cost of tuition. The reader of the Complete Guide to Christian Coach Training is responsible for verifying all information of interest directly with the training organizations.

THE ACADEMIES, INC.

Website	http://www.theacademies.com
Program Director	Susan Britton Whitcomb, PCC
Contact Name	Lyndsey Lehman, VP of Operations
Contact Email Address	lyndsey@theacademies.com
Contact Phone	(877) 659-3769 x4
Contact FAX	(888) 795-2725
Social Media Profiles	http://www.facebook.com/groups/theacademies/ http://twitter.com/#!/theacademies, @theacademies http://www.linkedin.com/groups?gid=1126187&mostPopular=&trk=tyah http://www.youtube.com/theacademies
DISTINCTIVES OF ORGANIZATION	The Academies, Inc. career coach Christian track is the only of its kind that approaches career calling, job transition and career management from a Biblical perspective. The program developer, best-selling author Susan Whitcomb, has penned seven career books, including The Christian's Career Journey.
Faculty Qualifications	ICF Professional Certified Coach, Certified Leadership Coach, Certified Career Management Coach, Certified Job Search Strategist, Certified Professional Christian Coach, Certified Personal Branding Strategist
Accredited by ICF	Accredited by ICF as ASCTH
Other Accreditation/Licensing	
BASIC COACHING SKILLS PROGRAM	**Certified Career Management Coach Program**
Year First Student Completed Training	2001
Number of months to complete	4 months
Technology Required	Phone; computer; Web; TV/DVD/CD
BASIC COACHING SKILLS COURSE(S)	
Training Hours	30 hours
Course Delivery Methods	Live Virtual Classroom Instruction, i.e. via phone and/or internet (100%)
BASIC COACHING SKILLS COMPLETION REQUIREMENTS	**Written Exam; Oral Exam; Being Coached**
Coaching Others Hours Required (Client)	Recommended, but none required
Being Coached Hours Required (Mentor)	5 hours
Number of Students Who Have Completed Requirements	363 Certified Career Management Coach Program including 96 for the Christian Track
Proprietary Course Materials	Proprietary Curriculum (400 pages) plus book: The Christian's Career Journey by Susan Britton Whitcomb
Additional Textbooks	CoActive Coaching (3rd edition) by Kimsey-House et al

BASIC COACHING SKILLS CERTIFICATION	**Certified Career Management Coach**
Additional Certification Requirements	None
Additional Certification Costs	None
Number of Certifications Awarded	278 for Certified Career Management Coach Program, including 64 for the Christian Track

BASIC COACHING SKILLS COSTS	
Estimated Cost of basic coaching skills training; includes multiple classes if applicable	$2897
Estimated Cost of Additional Books and Materials	$40
Estimated Cost of Required "Being Coached" hours	$750 - 1125
Additional Certification Costs	None
Other Costs	None
Total Cost Estimate	$3347 - $4022
Supplemental Cost Explanation	Price variation reflects possible early registration discount ($300) and choice of mentor coach for Being Coached Hours

ADVANCED OR NICHE-SPECIFIC TRAINING	
Advanced or Niche-Specific Training Described	The Academies offers additional programs for ongoing training, such as a 12-week Certified Job Search Strategist program, a 10-week Branded CareerCom Coach program, a 15-week Certified Leadership Coach program, and more. Niche training is offered via Social Media Career Strategist programs: Microblogging Career Strategist, Online Professional Networking Strategist, and Social Networking Career Strategist (each 6-sessions long).
ADDITIONAL INFORMATION	Career Coach Academy was established in 2001 with a core (secular) track for its Certified Career Management Coach (CCMC) program. In 2004, a Christian track for the CCMC career program was added. To further distinguish Christian tracks, Christian Coach Academy was added to The Academies in 2007.

The information on these profiles is subject to change at the discretion of the coach training organizations. This includes certification requirements and the cost of tuition. The reader of the Complete Guide to Christian Coach Training is responsible for verifying all information of interest directly with the training organizations.

WAY OF LIFE COACHING, LLC

Website	http://www.wayoflifecoaching.com
Program Director	Cheryl Scanlan
Contact Name	Cheryl Scanlan
Contact Email Address	Cheryl@wayoflifecoaching.com
Contact Phone	919.749.1800
Contact FAX	
Social Media Profiles	http://www.facebook.com/pages/Way-of-Life-Coaching-LLC/192279694148933
DISTINCTIVES OF ORGANIZATION	ACT! is taught by leadership developer and trainer, Cheryl Scanlan. ACT! is a highly interactive course that serves those new to coaching as well as experienced coaches. The course addresses ICF core competencies, examined from a Biblical worldview. Classes are sized to create an intimate, collaborative small group environment. Maximum class size is ten. Students have included pastors and ministry leaders.
Faculty Qualifications	PCC with 1000 hours of coaching.
Accredited by ICF	Approved by ICF for CCE's
Other Accreditation/Licensing	
BASIC COACHING SKILLS PROGRAM	ACT!
Year First Student Completed Training	2008
Number of months to complete	15 weeks
Technology Required	Phone; computer
BASIC COACHING SKILLS COURSE(S)	**ACT!**
Training Hours	30 hours
Course Delivery Methods	Live Virtual Classroom via phone and/or internet OR Live in-person 100%
BASIC COACHING SKILLS COMPLETION REQUIREMENTS	**Written Assignments; Oral Exam; Buddy/Triad Coaching;**
Coaching Others Hours Required (Client)	
Being Coached Hours Required (Mentor)	
Number of Students Who Have Completed Requirements	30
Proprietary Course Materials	120 color page workbook, developed with the visual learner in mind
Additional Textbooks	None, but suggested reading provided at the start of the course.

BASIC COACHING SKILLS CERTIFICATION	Certificate of Completion
Additional Certification Requirements	No
Additional Certification Costs	No
Number of Certifications Awarded	4

BASIC COACHING SKILLS COSTS	
Estimated Cost of basic coaching skills training; includes multiple classes if applicable	$600
Estimated Cost of Additional Books and Materials	$50
Estimated Cost of Required "Being Coached" hours	
Additional Certification Costs	
Other Costs	
Total Cost Estimate	$650
Supplemental Cost Explanation	No travel costs

ADVANCED OR NICHE-SPECIFIC TRAINING	
Advanced or Niche-Specific Training Described	
ADDITIONAL INFORMATION	The format of the classroom creates an intimate small group environment in which students collaborate and learn from each other as well as the material. Highly trained students have worked with new students. Training is intended to go beyond a download of information to further the acclimation and assimilation of the material. ACT! is taught via teleconference OR live and in person in Raleigh, NC.

The information on these profiles is subject to change at the discretion of the coach training organizations. This includes certification requirements and the cost of tuition. The reader of the Complete Guide to Christian Coach Training is responsible for verifying all information of interest directly with the training organizations.

WESTERN SEMINARY

Website	http://www.westerncoaching.com
Program Director	Chad Hall
Contact Name	Michelle Workman
Contact Email Address	mworkman@westernseminary.edu
Contact Phone	503-517-1912 Toll Free: 1-877-517-1800
Contact FAX	503-517-1889
Social Media Profiles	
DISTINCTIVES OF ORGANIZATION	Western Seminary offers coach training for new and experienced coaches seeking to grow in coaching competency. Classes are open to anyone, and are also available as graduate courses to seminarians pursuing an advanced degree. After taking Introduction to Coaching, students choose from 9 coach training classes, each offering 20 hours of coach specific training, plus a 12-hour supervision course. Classes are offered as 2-day intensives, live in person at any Western Seminary campus (Portland, OR; San Jose, CA; Sacramento, CA). All classes are designed to teach the ICF core coaching competencies.
Faculty Qualifications	A doctoral degree and/or ICF certification
Accredited by ICF	Accredited by ICF as ACSTH
Other Accreditation/Licensing	The Association of Theological Schools and the Northwest Commission on Colleges and Universities
BASIC COACHING SKILLS PROGRAM	**The Coaching Program at Western Seminary**
Year First Student Completed Training	2005
Number of months to complete	Varies by student, however the Certificate to Transformational Coaching can be completed in 18 months.
Technology Required	
BASIC COACHING SKILLS COURSE(S)	**Introduction to Coaching (MCS 510)**
Training Hours	20
Course Delivery Methods	In-Person (80%); Other (20%)
BASIC COACHING SKILLS COMPLETION REQUIREMENTS	**Written Assignments; Buddy/Triad Coaching**
Coaching Others Hours Required (Client)	Supervision class requires 25 hours of coaching others as pre-requisite.
Being Coached Hours Required (Mentor)	Varies depending on certification/degree track
Number of Students Who Have Completed Requirements	700+
Proprietary Course Materials	Each class contains proprietary student notes.
Additional Textbooks	Textbooks vary by class and are optional for Audit/Enrichment students. See www.westerncoaching.com/coaching-texts/ for required and recommended texts.

BASIC COACHING SKILLS CERTIFICATION	Certificate in Transformational Coaching
Additional Certification Requirements	The Certificate in Transformational Coaching (CTC) requires an advanced Training & Supervision phase (8 coaching classes and a coaching supervision class) and a Certification phase (6 observed mentor coaching sessions with written feedback, an oral exam and written exam).
Additional Certification Costs	Students taking classes for credit will pay higher tuition rates.
Number of Certifications Awarded	new program as of 2011
BASIC COACHING SKILLS COSTS	
Estimated Cost of basic coaching skills training; includes multiple classes if applicable	$375 - 445 per class
Estimated Cost of Additional Books and Materials	No text required for Audit/enrichment students; varies for Credit students by class
Estimated Cost of Required "Being Coached" hours	
Additional Certification Costs	
Other Costs	Travel costs if out of area
Total Cost Estimate	$375 - 445 per class plus travel (see below)
Supplemental Cost Explanation	Cost per class for Audit/Enrichment students (i.e. those pursuing the Certificate in Transformational Coaching) is $375 per class. Cost per class for student taking the class for academic credit is $445 per class. Total costs for Audit/Enrichment students pursuing the Certificate in Transformational Coaching which includes a Training & Supervision phase (8 coaching classes and 1 coaching supervision class) and a Certification phase (6 observed mentor coaching sessions, oral exam and written exam) is $4925. Students taking classes for credit will pay higher tuition rates.
ADVANCED OR NICHE-SPECIFIC TRAINING	
Advanced or Niche-Specific Training Described	**MCS 510**: Intro to Coaching is a pre-requisite for each of these classes: **MCS 511**: Coaching for Change; **MCS 512**: Life and Personal Coaching; **MCS 513**: Coach Approach to Leading and Managing; **MCS 514**: Coaching in Congregations for Spiritual Formation; **MCS 515**: Coaching and a Brain-based Approach to Learning; **MCS 516**: Using Assessments, Inventories & Tools in Coaching; **MCS 517**: The Language of Coaching; **MCS 518**: Growing Your Coaching Practice; **MCS 519**: Coaching Supervision
GRAD SCHOOL INFORMATION	Degrees and Certificates offered are Master of Arts in Ministry and Leadership - Coaching Track, Graduate Studies Certificate, and Certificate in Transformational Coaching.
ADDITIONAL INFORMATION	Find four training options at the following link: http://westerncoaching.com/training-options/ Live training on site locations include Western Seminary Campuses in Portland, OR, San Jose, CA, and Sacramento, CA.

The information on these profiles is subject to change at the discretion of the coach training organizations. This includes certification requirements and the cost of tuition. The reader of the Complete Guide to Christian Coach Training is responsible for verifying all information of interest directly with the training organization.

WORKPLACE COACH INSTITUTE, INC.

Website	www.workplacecoachinstitute.com
Program Director	Nancy Branton, MA, PCC
Contact Name	Nancy Branton, MA, PCC
Contact Email Address	nancy@workplacecoachinstitute.com
Contact Phone	800-691-2553
Contact FAX	800-778-3582
Social Media Profiles	http://twitter.com/#!/wcicoach https://www.facebook.com/group.php?gid=161498523866213&ref=ts http://www.linkedin.com/groups?gid=3327223&about
DISTINCTIVES OF ORGANIZATION	The Christian Leadership and Talent Management Coach Training Program, developed by executive coach Nancy Branton, PCC, equips leaders and internal and external coaches with solid leadership development and talent management tools, as well as the ability to coach and support marketplace Christians as they live out their faith in the workplace.
Faculty Qualifications	Required to hold ICF's Professional Certified Coach credential and must have completed the Leadership and Talent Management Coach training program.
Accredited by ICF	Accredited by ICF as an ACSTH
Other Accreditation/Licensing	This program is approved by The Center for Credentialing Education (CCE) towards their Board Certified Coach (BCC) credential. Also, it is approved by the Human Resources Certification Institute (HRCI) for recertification CEUS.
BASIC COACHING SKILLS PROGRAM	**Certified Leadership and Talent Management Coach Training Program (CLTMC)**
Year First Student Completed Training	2006
Number of months to complete	4 months
Technology Required	Phone; Computer; Internet
BASIC COACHING SKILLS COURSE(S)	**Certified Leadership and Talent Management Coach (CLTMC) Training Program**
Training Hours	30 hours
Course Delivery Methods	Live, In-Person (100%); Upon request, we bring this training onsite. Students may be part of a cohort or be taught individually.
BASIC COACHING SKILLS COMPLETION REQUIREMENTS	**Written Exam, Buddy or Triad Coaching, Coaching Others**
Coaching Others Hours Required (Client)	5
Being Coached Hours Required (Mentor)	
Number of Students Who Have Completed Requirements	145 (32 from Christian Track)

Proprietary Course Materials	Leadership & Talent Management Coach Binder Materials and Forms; People Management Primer: Coaching Leaders to be Principled and Create Thriving Workplaces; 15 Biblical Building Blocks of a Transformational Leader Model with Scriptures
Additional Textbooks	
BASIC COACHING SKILLS CERTIFICATION	**Certified Leadership and Talent Management Coach - Christian Church/Business Leader OR Certified Leadership and Talent Management Coach - Christian Coach**
Additional Certification Requirements	Five mentor coaching sessions and completion of a Client Case Study that includes five, 45-minute sessions with a client.
Additional Certification Costs	$750 for five mentor coaching sessions.
Number of Certifications Awarded	74

BASIC COACHING SKILLS COSTS	
Estimated Cost of basic coaching skills training; includes multiple classes if applicable	$3200 or $2900 with early registration
Estimated Cost of Additional Books and Materials	$10.19
Estimated Cost of Required "Being Coached" hours	
Additional Certification Costs	$750
Other Costs	
Total Cost Estimate	$3960.19 with early registration

Supplemental Cost Explanation	
ADVANCED OR NICHE-SPECIFIC TRAINING	
Advanced or Niche-Specific Training Described	
ADDITIONAL INFORMATION	Students can complete this course completely by distance learning, but it can also be taught on-site and can be customized. Students have the option to become certified in three leadership assessments and that cost is $500.

The information on these profiles is subject to change at the discretion of the coach training organizations. This includes certification requirements and the cost of tuition. The reader of the Complete Guide to Christian Coach Training is responsible for verifying all information of interest directly with the training organization.

SECTION 5: TOOLS AND RESOURCES

Table of Contents

***Eleven Factors Worksheet** - (for use with Section Three, pp. 17-26)*

1. Ask yourself: *Is it coaching or something else? (p. 17)*

____

____

____

____

____

____

____

____

2. Ask yourself: *Do I want to be the coach without the training? (p.17)*

____

____

____

____

____

____

____

____

3. Ask yourself: *Is secular coach training an option? (p. 18)*

____

____

____

____

____

____

____

____

4. Ask yourself: Do I want accredited training or not? (p. 19)

5. Ask yourself: *What type of certification do I want to receive?* *(p.21)*

6. Ask yourself: *Do I need "niche" or specialized training?* *(p. 24)*

7. Ask yourself: *What training logistics are ideal for me? (p. 24)*

8. Ask yourself: *What will I pay for coach training? (p. 24)*

9. Ask yourself: *What makes a training program excellent? (p. 25)*

10. Ask yourself: *How important are coaching community connections?* (p. 25)

11. Ask yourself: *Does this program feel like a good match?* (p. 26)

Lord, help me be sensitive to your leading as I consider, with you, if this program is the "right fit" for me.

Prayers of a Christ-Centered Coach

Lord, thank you for calling me to be a coach.

- Let your unconditional love flow through me.
- Spotlight my sins that encumber.
- Mold me into a servant leader.

Before each coaching conversation, I pray

- for boldness to be your ambassador
- for the ones I'm coaching to listen to you
- for your direction, insights, and inspiration to take action.

During each coaching conversation, I pray

- for guidance from you on what to say and how to say it
- for wisdom to know when to turn the conversation into a time of prayer
- for peace when it is time to be silent and let you do all the speaking

And beyond each coaching conversation, I pray

- for fears of the unknown to be calmed
- for you to fill in the gaps of what was not said and what was really needed beyond the surface
- for boldness to take actions that go beyond what we know how to do and outcomes we know we can control
- for followers of you, Lord, and not followers of the coach
- for Christian coaches and their global impact
- for coaches everywhere who are making the ground fertile for the gospel

May You be the one who is glorified in all we say and do.

In Jesus' name, Amen.

Creswell, Jane. Christ-centered Coaching: 7 Benefits for Ministry Leaders. St. Louis, MO: Chalice Press, 2006. Print. Page 137. Used by permission

Bible Verses for Coaches and Clients

I came so they can have real and eternal life,
more and better life than they ever dreamed of.
John 10:10 (The Message)

Thy word is a lamp unto my feet,
and a light unto my path.
Psalm 119:105 (KJV)

God doesn't want us to be shy with his gifts,
but bold and loving and sensible.
2 Timothy 1:7 (The Message)

His divine power has given us
everything we need for life and godliness.
2 Peter 1:3 (NIV)

Where there is no vision, the people perish.
Proverbs 29:18 (KJV)

Love the Lord your God with all your heart
and with all your soul and with all your mind.
This is the first and greatest commandment
and the second is like it:
Love your neighbor as yourself.
Matthew 22:37-39 (NIV)

Delight yourself in the LORD
and he will give you the desires of your heart.
Psalm 37:4 (NIV)

The purposes of the human heart are deep waters,
but those who have insight draw them out.
Proverbs 20:5 (TNIV)

Stand at the crossroads and look;
ask for the ancient paths, ask where the good way is,
and walk in it, and you will find rest for your souls.
Jeremiah 6:16 (NIV)

I am the way, the truth and the life.
John 14:6 (NIV)

God rewrote the text of my life
when I opened the book of my heart to his eyes.
Psalm 18:24 (The Message)

Ways to Discern Opportunities

The following is available at the Christian Coaches Network website (www.christiancoaches.com), and is helpful information for coaches to consider.

As coaching for Christians becomes better known, a fertile ground is provided for opportunists.

Sometimes, opportunities arise to be involved in coaching companies, training situations, speaking engagements, media opportunities, etc. Some are great - others are not. Here are some guidelines and things to watch for that may be helpful in making decisions that you will not later regret.

1. Pray for discernment and wisdom as you read. When you hit a red flag, don't waste time reading further.

2. Just because it sounds Christian, doesn't mean it is. Dig. Anyone can use Christian terms and coaching catchwords in the same sentence. Check for substance.

3. Always check the identity of the person heading up the organization. If you can't find the information, or have a lot of trouble locating the owner or CEO, consider that a red flag. Who are other stakeholders?

4. Look for contradictions, marketing hype, promises of fame and fortune and unsubstantiated statements. Remember the old saying: "If it sounds too good to be true, it probably is."

5. Consider the qualifications and credentials of the person making the offer. If it's a coaching situation, are there recognized organizations behind this person either in coach training, ICF, accredited university or through a group with credentialed leadership that has an excellent reputation? Does this person have a clear understanding of the legalities, ethics and differences between coaching, consulting and counseling? If you are going to put your reputation on the line, you want to be very certain it is not tarnished by association.

6. Be assertive in asking for references and ways to verify what you are being told.

7. If you are checking a website, follow all the links.

8. Look for empty promises being offered to you and also to the public. Credibility begins with legitimacy.

9. Look through the sales pitch carefully. If they are asking you for money or a substantial amount of time, check carefully to determine competitive value and if there is a wiggle clause. Is what they are offering solid, viable and credible?

10. Guarantees, certification and accreditation are only as credible as the person or organization granting them.

11. Determine your ROI (return on investment). What is the cost, what is the potential payoff? How much of your time is involved? How much financial risk is involved? If it is a media opportunity, what are the demographics? Does the media reach the market that contain your potential ideal clients?

12. Pay attention to how much or little of God's peace you sense around the opportunity. If you still aren't sure, ask someone you trust.

The Complete Guide to Christian Coach Training

Definitions and Standards

In order to establish standards for ***The Complete Guide to Christian Coach Training***, the following provides definitions of coaching, key skills and ethical standards. The coaching training programs featured in the Guide were asked to review and confirm their alignment with these definitions and standards.

DEFINITION OF COACHING

In his ground breaking book, *Christian Coaching: Helping Others Turn Potential Into Reality* (2001), Christian leader **Gary R. Collins** defines coaching as "the art and practice of guiding a person or group from where they are toward the greater competence and fulfillment that they desire."

Tony Stoltzfus, coach trainer and author of *Leadership Coaching: The Disciplines, Skills and Heart of a Christian Coach* (2005), says that coaching conversations are based on the premise that "the best way to help you change is to create a structured, supportive relationship that helps you take responsibility for your life and make the changes you want to make."

In ***The Journal of Psychology and Christianity***, **Dr. Fred Craigie** edits the presentation, ***A Crash Course in Christian Coaching***, by coach trainer and pioneer in the field of Christian coaching, **Christopher McCluskey**. The distinctives of coaching are summarized this way:

> Coaching also differs from other helping relationships, such as mentoring, discipleship, consulting, managing, and spiritual formation. All of these relationships have a common element, which is that the facilitator works with the client from the outside in. If you are mentoring someone, you as the master have the ability and expertise which the apprentice lacks. Your role is to infuse that ability and expertise into the inner person of the apprentice. It is outside of the experience of the apprentice and the goal is to bring it in. Similarly, if you are discipling someone, you are the mature person in the faith and your goal is to infuse into the disciple the basic tenants of the faith... moral codes, spiritual disciplines and so forth... which they do not presently have. Your goal is to get them to the point where they can follow on their own the process of sanctification and growing. If you are a consultant or a manager, you are the person with the expertise which is brought to a situation which lacks that level of understanding. Even with spiritual formation... which shares the goal of supporting people in their response to God's calling... spiritual directors typically are more mature in the faith, have studied more extensively and often play more directive and didactic roles with people.
>
> Coaching, in contrast, is about drawing from what is inside the person and helping to flesh it out to their outer person. "What would it look like," I ask, "if you began living out more of what you say is in there?" Rather than an expert, the role of the coach is to be a facilitator, a prober/questioner, a clarifier, an encourager, a challenger, an accountability partner and ultimately, a conduit for the Holy Spirit.

Finally, the **International Coach Federation** (ICF), the oldest and largest professional association of coaches worldwide - though certainly not a Christian organization - has undeniably shaped the profession of coaching in our world.

The ICF defines professional coaching as follows:

- Coaching is partnering with clients in a thought-provoking and creative process that inspires them to maximize their personal and professional potential.
- Professional coaches provide an ongoing partnership designed to help clients produce fulfilling results in their personal and professional lives.
- Coaches help people improve their performances and enhance the quality of their lives.
- Coaches are trained to listen, to observe and to customize their approach to individual client needs. They seek to elicit solutions and strategies from the client; they believe the client is naturally creative and resourceful. The coach's job is to provide support to enhance the skills, resources, and creativity that the client already has.

Key Coaching Skills

To be included in The Complete Guide to Christian Coach Training, training programs are NOT required to be affiliated with ICF currently or in the future. However, coach training programs are asked to review the following key coaching skills, referenced here in the ICF core competencies, and determine if this describes the coaching skills taught in the coach training program.

*** DISREGARD REFERENCES TO THE ICF STANDARDS OF CONDUCT AND ICF ETHICAL GUIDELINES IN SECTION A.1.a. AND A.1.b. Though Christian coach training programs may be comfortable with ICF guidelines, for the purposes of The Complete Guide to Christian Coach Training, guidelines and standards are provided below that reflect a Christian worldview, acknowledging Christ as the ultimate authority and guide for all things, including our professional endeavors.

A. SETTING THE FOUNDATION

1. Meeting Ethical Guidelines and Professional Standards -

Understanding of coaching ethics and standards and ability to apply them appropriately in all coaching situations

a. Understands and exhibits in own behaviors the ICF Standards of Conduct***
b. Understands and follows all ICF Ethical Guidelines***
c. Clearly communicates the distinctions between coaching, consulting, psychotherapy and other support professions

d. Refers client to another support professional as needed, knowing when this is needed and the available resources

2. Establishing the Coaching Agreement - Ability to understand what is required in the specific coaching interaction and to come to agreement with the prospective and new client about the coaching process and relationship

a. Understands and effectively discusses with the client the guidelines and specific parameters of the coaching relationship (e.g., logistics, fees, scheduling, inclusion of others if appropriate)
b. Reaches agreement about what is appropriate in the relationship and what is not, what is and is not being offered, and about the client's and coach's responsibilities
c. Determines whether there is an effective match between his/her coaching method and the needs of the prospective client

B. CO-CREATING THE RELATIONSHIP

3. Establishing Trust and Intimacy with the Client - Ability to create a safe, supportive environment that produces ongoing mutual respect and trust

a. Shows genuine concern for the client's welfare and future
b. Continuously demonstrates personal integrity, honesty and sincerity
c. Establishes clear agreements and keeps promises
d. Demonstrates respect for client's perceptions, learning style, personal being
e. Provides ongoing support for and champions new behaviors and actions, including those involving risk taking and fear of failure
f. Asks permission to coach client in sensitive, new areas

4. Coaching Presence - Ability to be fully conscious and create spontaneous relationship with the client, employing a style that is open, flexible and confident

a. Is present and flexible during the coaching process, dancing in the moment
b. Accesses own intuition and trusts one's inner knowing - "goes with the gut"
c. Is open to not knowing and takes risks
d. Sees many ways to work with the client, and chooses in the moment what is most effective
e. Uses humor effectively to create lightness and energy
f. Confidently shifts perspectives and experiments with new possibilities for own action
g. Demonstrates confidence in working with strong emotions, and can self-manage and not be overpowered or enmeshed by client's emotions

C. COMMUNICATING EFFECTIVELY

5. Active Listening - Ability to focus completely on what the client is saying and is not saying, to understand the meaning of what is said in the context of the client's desires, and to support client self-expression

a. Attends to the client and the client's agenda, and not to the coach's agenda for the client
b. Hears the client's concerns, goals, values and beliefs about what is and is not possible
c. Distinguishes between the words, the tone of voice, and the body language
d. Summarizes, paraphrases, reiterates, mirrors back what client has said to ensure clarity and understanding
e. Encourages, accepts, explores and reinforces the client's expression of feelings, perceptions, concerns

f. Integrates and builds on client's ideas and suggestions
g. "Bottom-lines" or understands the essence of the client's communication and helps the client get there rather than engaging in long descriptive stories
h. Allows the client to vent or "clear" the situation without judgment or attachment in order to move on to next steps

6. Powerful Questioning -Ability to ask questions that reveal the information needed for maximum benefit to the coaching relationship and the client

a. Asks questions that reflect active listening and an understanding of the client's perspective
b. Asks questions that evoke discovery, insight, commitment or action (e.g., those that challenge the client's assumptions)
c. Asks open-ended questions that create greater clarity, possibility or new learning
d. Asks questions that move the client towards what they desire, not questions that ask for the client to justify or look backwards

7. Direct Communication - Ability to communicate effectively during coaching sessions, and to use language that has the greatest positive impact on the client

a. Is clear, articulate and direct in sharing and providing feedback
b. Reframes and articulates to help the client understand from another perspective what he/she wants or is uncertain about
c. Clearly states coaching objectives, meeting agenda, purpose of techniques or exercises
d. Uses language appropriate and respectful to the client (e.g., non-sexist, non-racist, non-technical, non-jargon)
e. Uses metaphor and analogy to help to illustrate a point or paint a verbal picture

D. FACILITATING LEARNING AND RESULTS

8. Creating Awareness - Ability to integrate and accurately evaluate multiple sources of information, and to make interpretations that help the client to gain awareness and thereby achieve agreed-upon results

a. Goes beyond what is said in assessing client's concerns, not getting hooked by the client's description
b. Invokes inquiry for greater understanding, awareness and clarity
c. Identifies for the client his/her underlying concerns, typical and fixed ways of perceiving himself/herself and the world, differences between the facts and the interpretation, disparities between thoughts, feelings and action
d. Helps clients to discover for themselves the new thoughts, beliefs,

perceptions, emotions, moods, etc. that strengthen their ability to take action and achieve what is important to them

e. Communicates broader perspectives to clients and inspires commitment to shift their viewpoints and find new possibilities for action
f. Helps clients to see the different, interrelated factors that affect them and their behaviors (e.g., thoughts, emotions, body, background)
g. Expresses insights to clients in ways that are useful and meaningful for the client
h. Identifies major strengths vs. major areas for learning and growth, and what is most important to address during coaching
i. Asks the client to distinguish between trivial and significant issues, situational vs. recurring behaviors, when detecting a separation between what is being stated and what is being done

9. Designing Actions - Ability to create with the client opportunities for ongoing learning, during coaching and in work/life situations, and for taking new actions that will most effectively lead to agreed-upon coaching results

a. Brainstorms and assists the client to define actions that will enable the client to demonstrate, practice and deepen new learning
b. Helps the client to focus on and systematically explore specific concerns and opportunities that are central to agreed-upon coaching goals
c. Engages the client to explore alternative ideas and solutions, to evaluate options, and to make related decisions
d. Promotes active experimentation and self-discovery, where the client applies what has been discussed and learned during sessions immediately afterwards in his/her work or life setting
e. Celebrates client successes and capabilities for future growth
f. Challenges client's assumptions and perspectives to provoke new ideas and find new possibilities for action
g. Advocates or brings forward points of view that are aligned with client goals and, without attachment, engages the client to consider them
h. Helps the client "Do It Now" during the coaching session, providing immediate support
i. Encourages stretches and challenges but also a comfortable pace of learning

10. Planning and Goal Setting - Ability to develop and maintain an effective coaching plan with the client

a. Consolidates collected information and establishes a coaching plan and development goals with the client that address concerns and major areas for learning and development
b. Creates a plan with results that are attainable, measurable, specific and have target dates
c. Makes plan adjustments as warranted by the coaching process and by changes in the situation
d. Helps the client identify and access different resources for learning

(e.g., books, other professionals)

e. Identifies and targets early successes that are important to the client

11. Managing Progress and Accountability - Ability to hold attention on what is important for the client, and to leave responsibility with the client to take action

a. Clearly requests of the client actions that will move the client toward their stated goals
b. Demonstrates follow through by asking the client about those actions that the client committed to during the previous session(s)
c. Acknowledges the client for what they have done, not done, learned or become aware of since the previous coaching session(s)
d. Effectively prepares, organizes and reviews with client information obtained during sessions
e. Keeps the client on track between sessions by holding attention on the coaching plan and outcomes, agreed-upon courses of action, and topics for future session(s)
f. Focuses on the coaching plan but is also open to adjusting behaviors and actions based on the coaching process and shifts in direction during sessions
g. Is able to move back and forth between the big picture of where the client is heading, setting a context for what is being discussed and where the client wishes to go
h. Promotes client's self-discipline and holds the client accountable for what they say they are going to do, for the results of an intended action, or for a specific plan with related time frames
i. Develops the client's ability to make decisions, address key concerns, and develop himself/herself (to get feedback, to determine priorities and set the pace of learning, to reflect on and learn from experiences)
j. Positively confronts the client with the fact that he/she did not take agreed-upon actions

CODE OF ETHICS AND STANDARDS OF PROFESSIONAL CONDUCT

The following code of ethics and professional standards is that of the Christian Coaches Network. CCN has been connecting the diverse community of Christian coaches since 1998 and is a welcoming place for those that name Christ as their Lord and Savior and live intentionally to reflect the teachings of the Bible. FOR THE PURPOSES OF *THE COMPLETE GUIDE TO CHRISTIAN COACH TRAINING, 2010 EDITION*, TRAINING PROGRAMS ARE NOT REQUIRED TO AFFILIATE WITH CCN. As such, training programs may disregard the references to CCN in numbers 10 and 11 below.

As a Christian Coach:

1. I hold myself accountable to the highest level of integrity, honoring Jesus Christ individually and corporately, in all my associations with clients and colleagues.
2. I will maintain complete confidentiality with my clients, within the confines of the law.
3. I will be clear with my clients about the nature of the coaching relationship, including structure, fees, refunds, expectations and guarantees.
4. I will never give a client's name to anyone, for any purpose, without express permission.
5. I will give credit where credit is due for materials supplied by other sources, respecting copyrights, trademarks and intellectual property.
6. I will judiciously avoid conflicts of interest. If any should arise, I shall, without delay, inform concerned parties of my position.
7. I will represent myself honestly and clearly to my clients, and coach only within my areas of expertise.
8. I will actively pursue well being, wholeness, and continual learning in my own life.
9. I will refer a client to another coach if I am not within my area of expertise or comfort, so the client gets the best possible coaching.
10. I will honor my Christian values in my professional conduct, placing neither blame nor blemish on the name of Christ, the Christian Coaches Network or the coaching profession.
11. I will support the Christian Coaches Network to further professional coaching among believers.

Christian Coaches Network, www.christiancoaches.com

SECTION SIX: CHRISTIAN COACH TRAINING PROGRAMS GALLERY

Finally, in an effort to provide you with more of the personality of each of the Christian coach training programs profiled in The Guide, I asked each school to provide a graphic for the Gallery. Each image has a page reference to the profile in The Guide as well as being linked directly to the website.

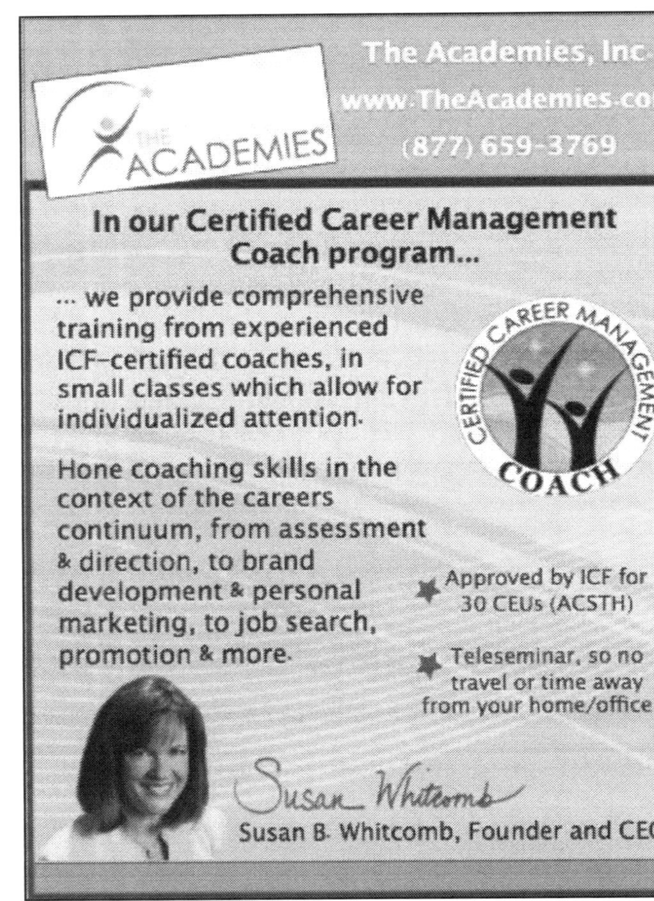

THE ACADEMIES
More information on page 63

DREAM MENTORS
More information on page 47

LEVERAGE THE POWER OF TRANSFORMATIONAL COACHING... ACHIEVE EXCELLENCE.

CENTER FOR COACHING EXCELLENCE

Whether you want professional coach training to launch a new career or desire to incorporate coaching into your organizational cl mate... our coach trainings equip you with the values and competencies you will need for maximum impact.

Our comprehensive program includes:

- ICF compliant training
- Values-based training
- Transformational training methodology
- Certified ICF PCC trainers
- Distinctive on-campus workshops & telesessions
- Affordable tuition

For more information visit: www.centerforcoachingexcellence.com

CENTER FOR COACHING EXCELLENCE

More information on page 33

COACHNET GLOBAL

More information on page 43

ASSEMBLIES OF GOD THEOLOGICAL SEMINARY

More information on page 31

LIFEFORMING LEADERSHIP

More information on page 57

WAY OF LIFE COACHING
More information on page 65

LIFE BREAKTHROUGH ACADEMY
More information on page 53

LIFE PURPOSE COACHING CENTERS INTERNATIONAL®

More information on page 55

INSTITUTE FOR LIFE COACH TRAINING

More information on page 51

COACH APPROACH MINISTRIES
More information on page 37

COACHING4CLERGY
More information on page 39

SOUTHWESTERN CHRISTIAN UNIVERSITY

more information on page 61

CREATIVE RESULTS MANAGEMENT

More information on page 45

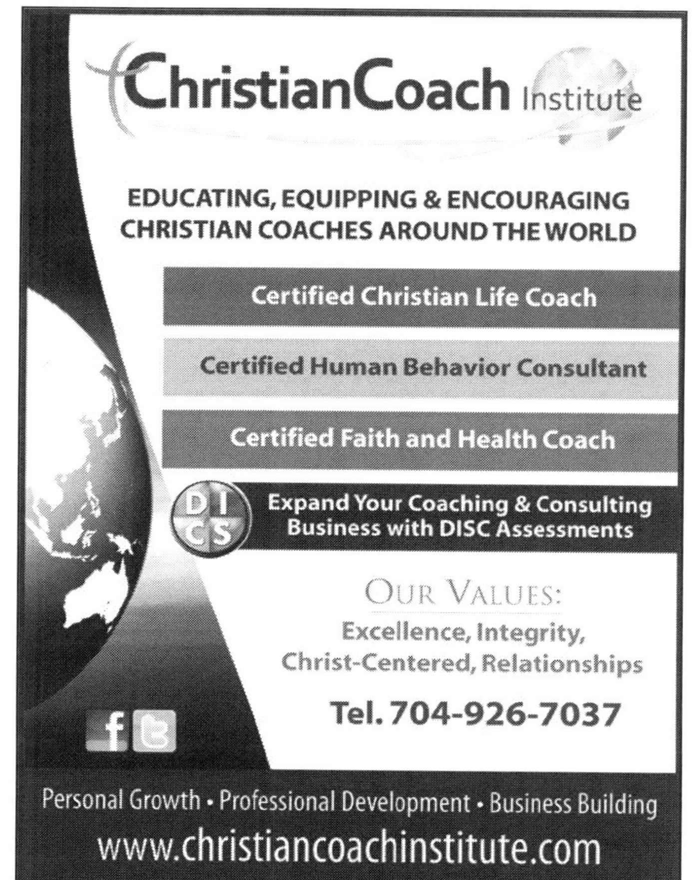

CHRISTIAN COACH INSTITUTE
More information on page 35

WORKPLACE COACH INSTITUTE
More information on page 69

ERICKSON COLLEGE INTERNATIONAL

More information on page 49

COACHING MISSION INTERNATIONAL

More information on page 41

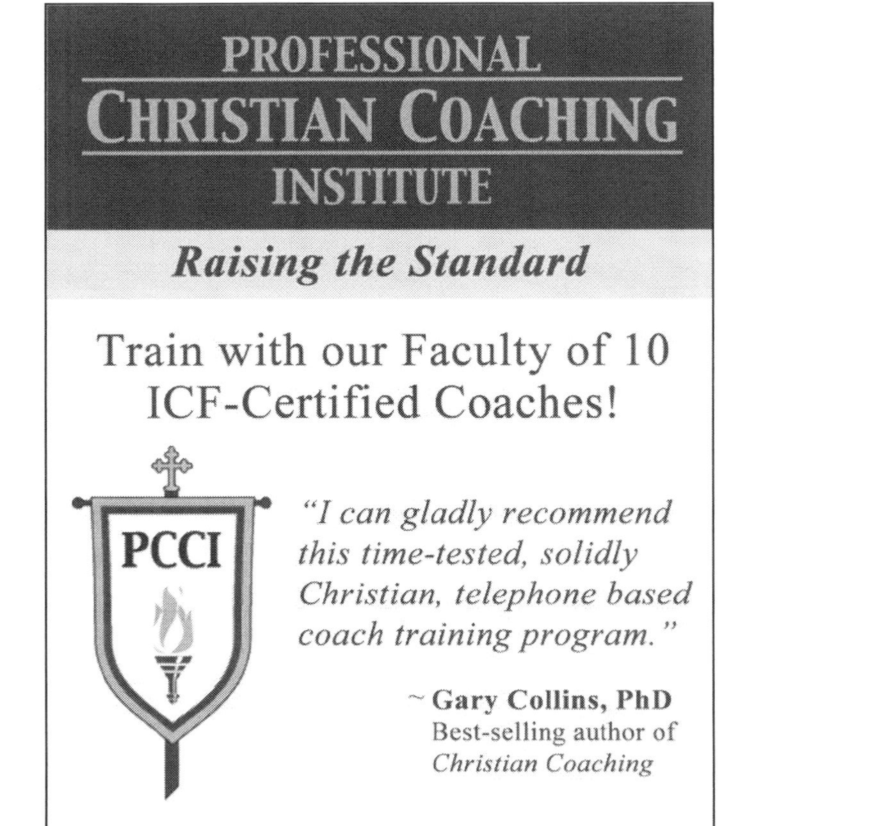

PROFESSIONAL CHRISTIAN COACHING INSTITUTE

More information on page 59

WESTERN SEMINARY

More information on page 67

Made in the USA
Lexington, KY
11 January 2012